This is Man!

Peter Slater

Exercise to live. Never live
to exercise.
Jack LaLanne

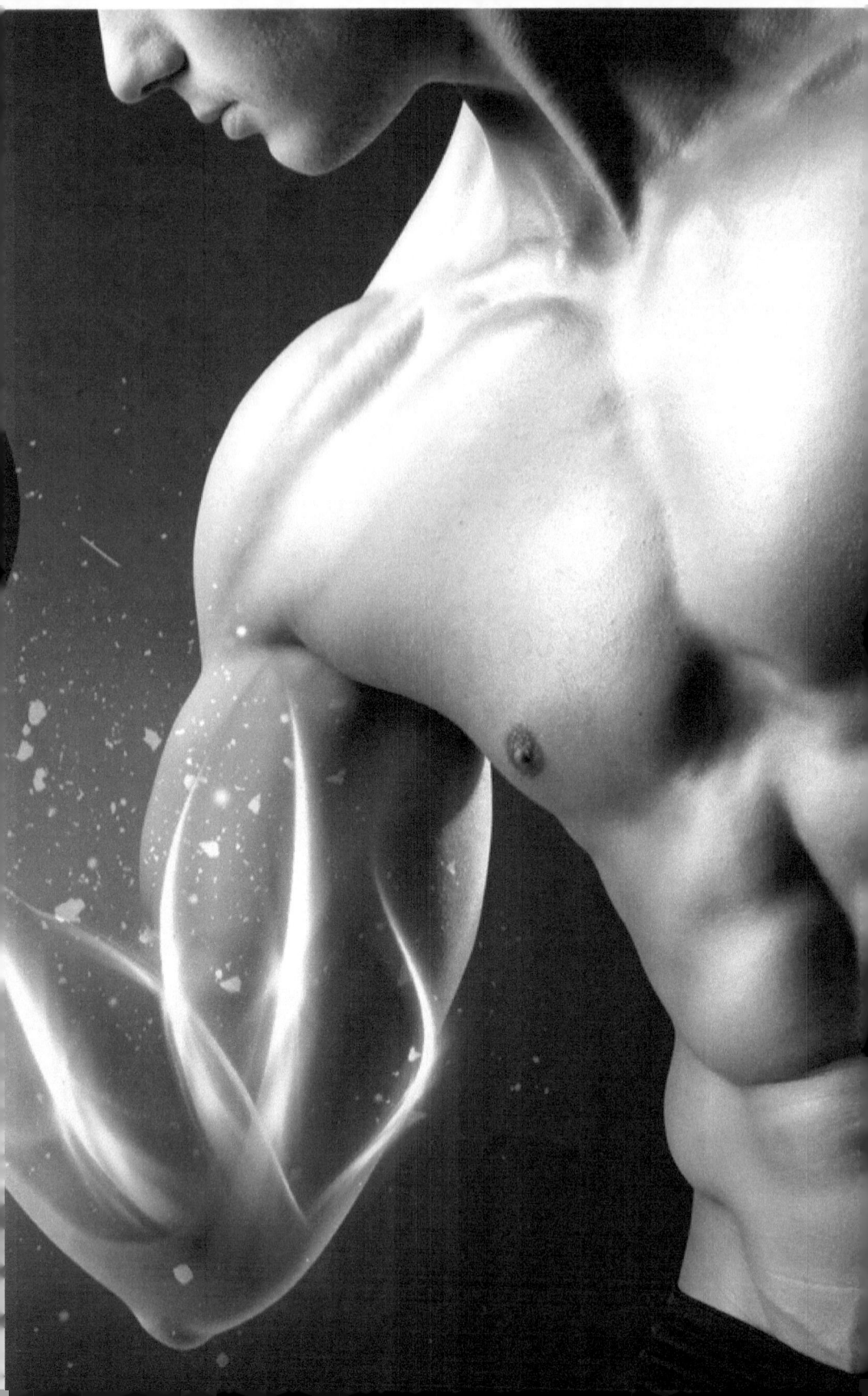

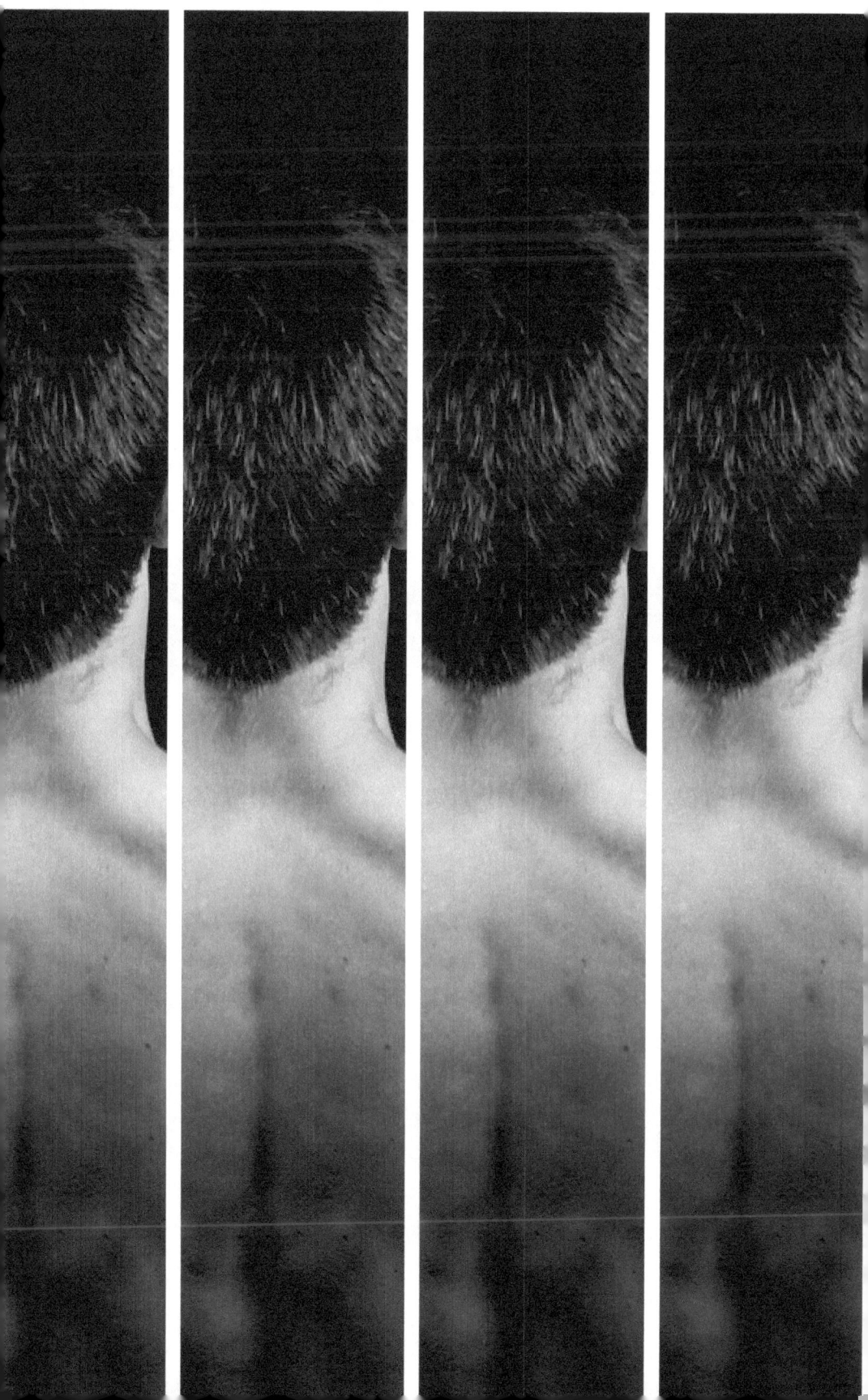

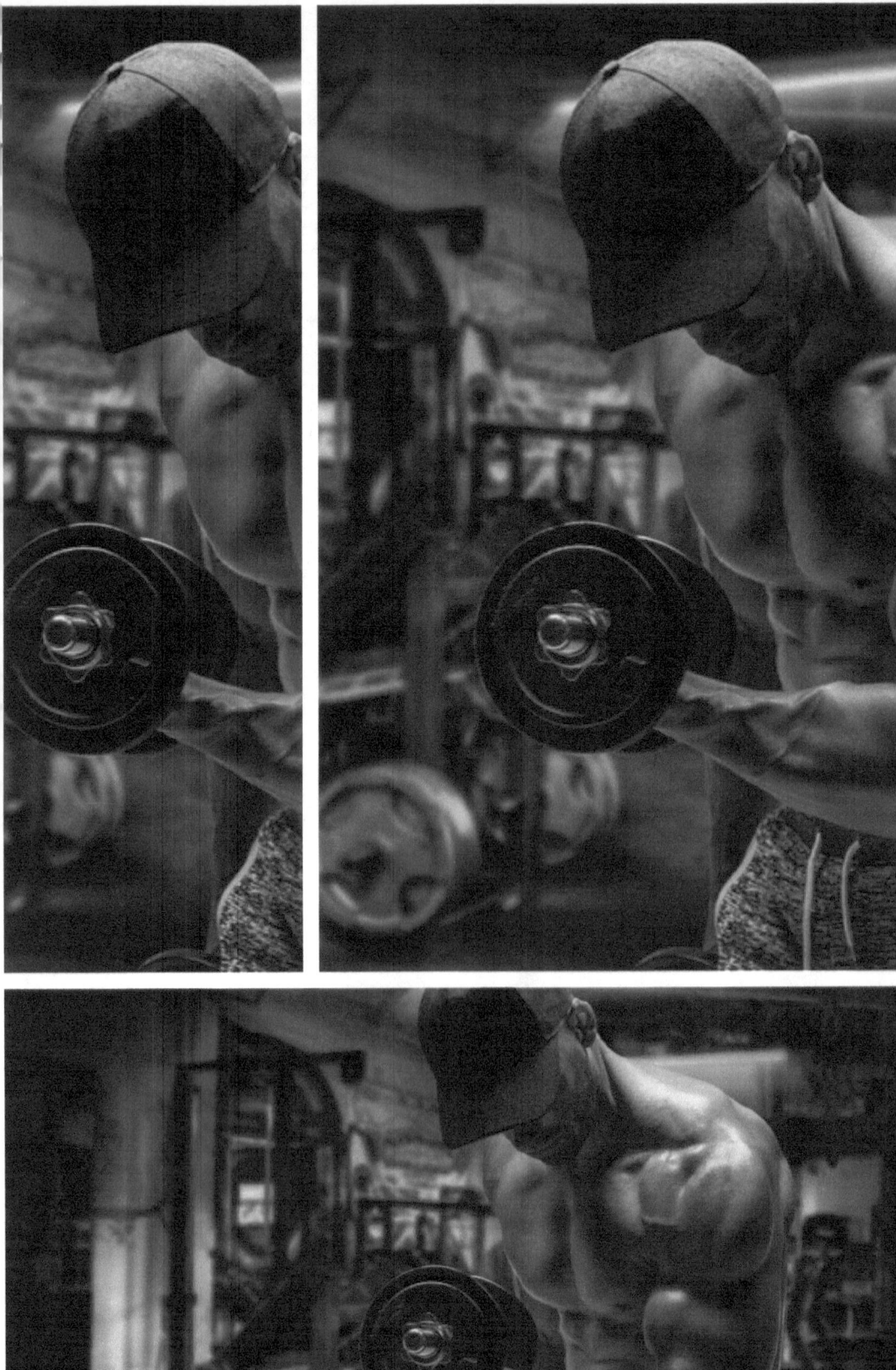

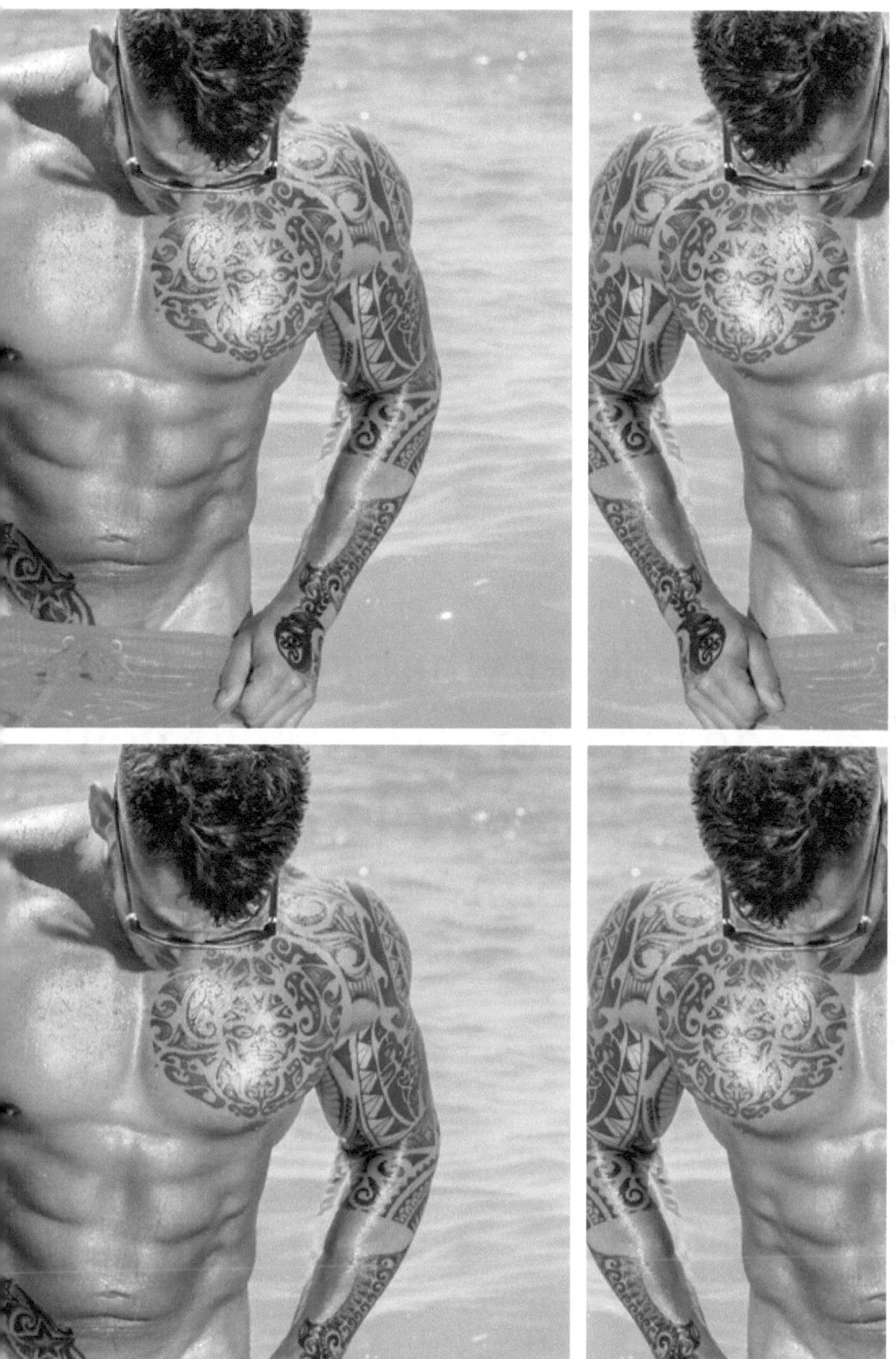

Do not let what you cannot do interfere with what you can do.
John Wooden

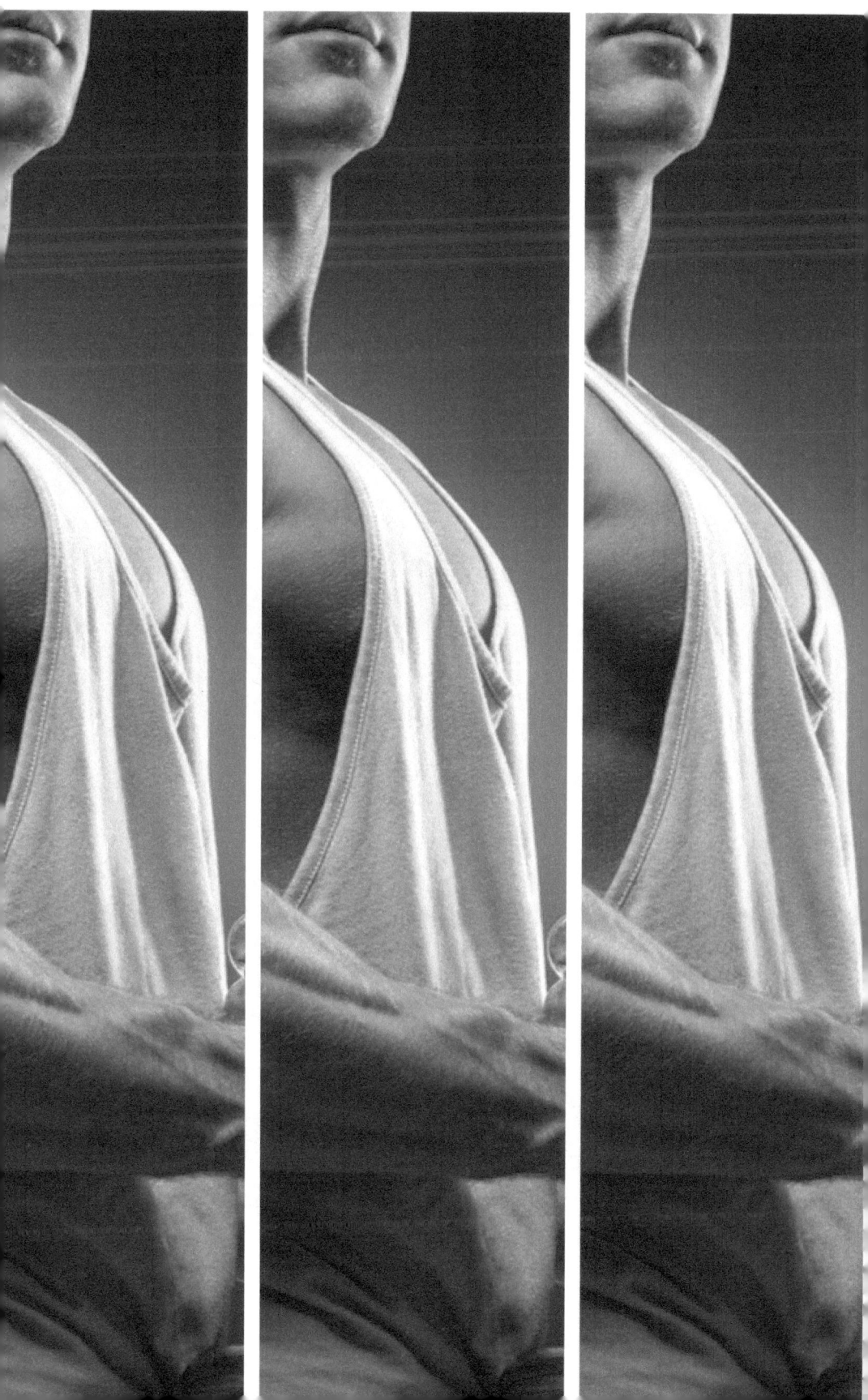

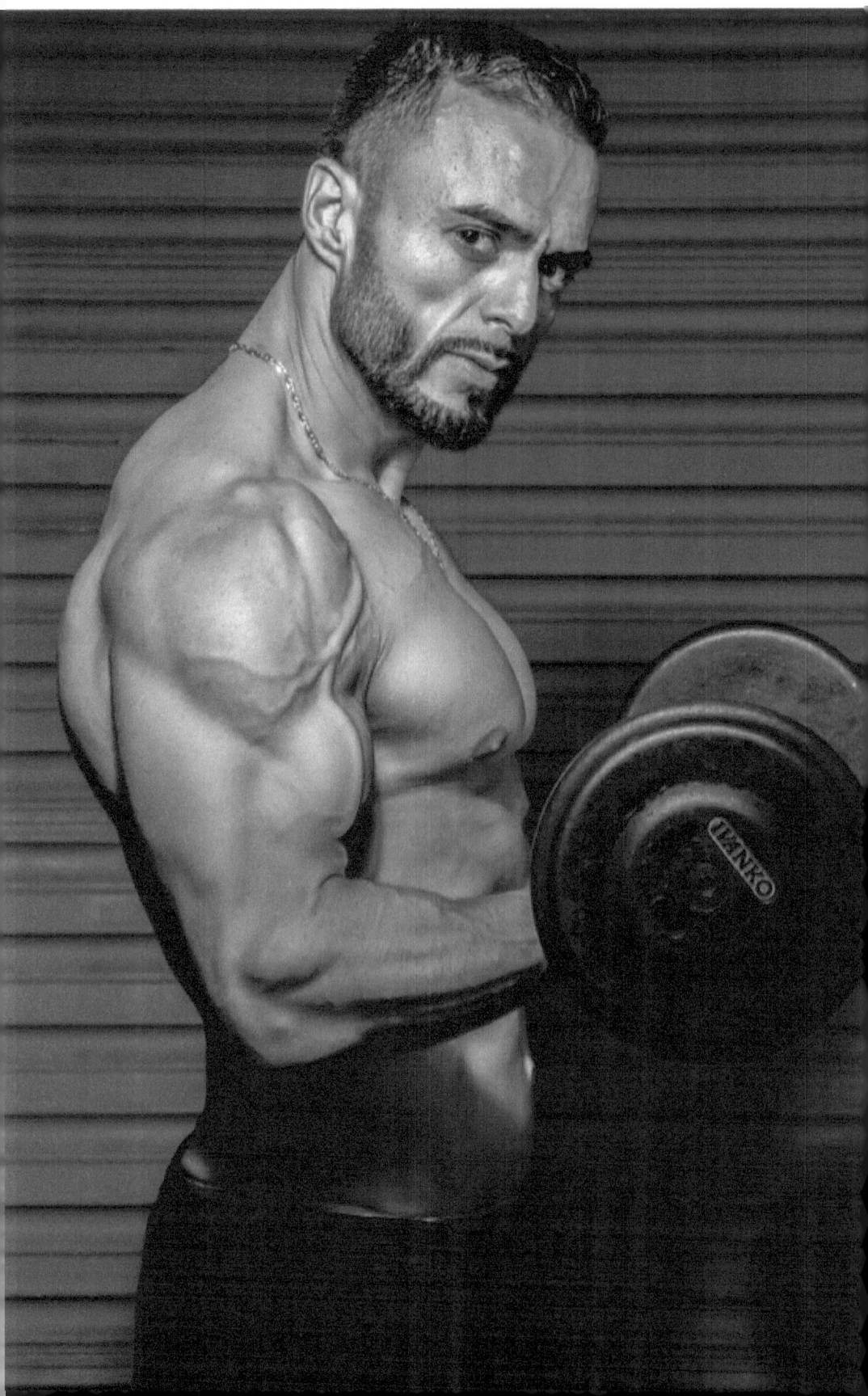

No matter how good you get you can always get better, and that's the exciting part.Tiger Woods

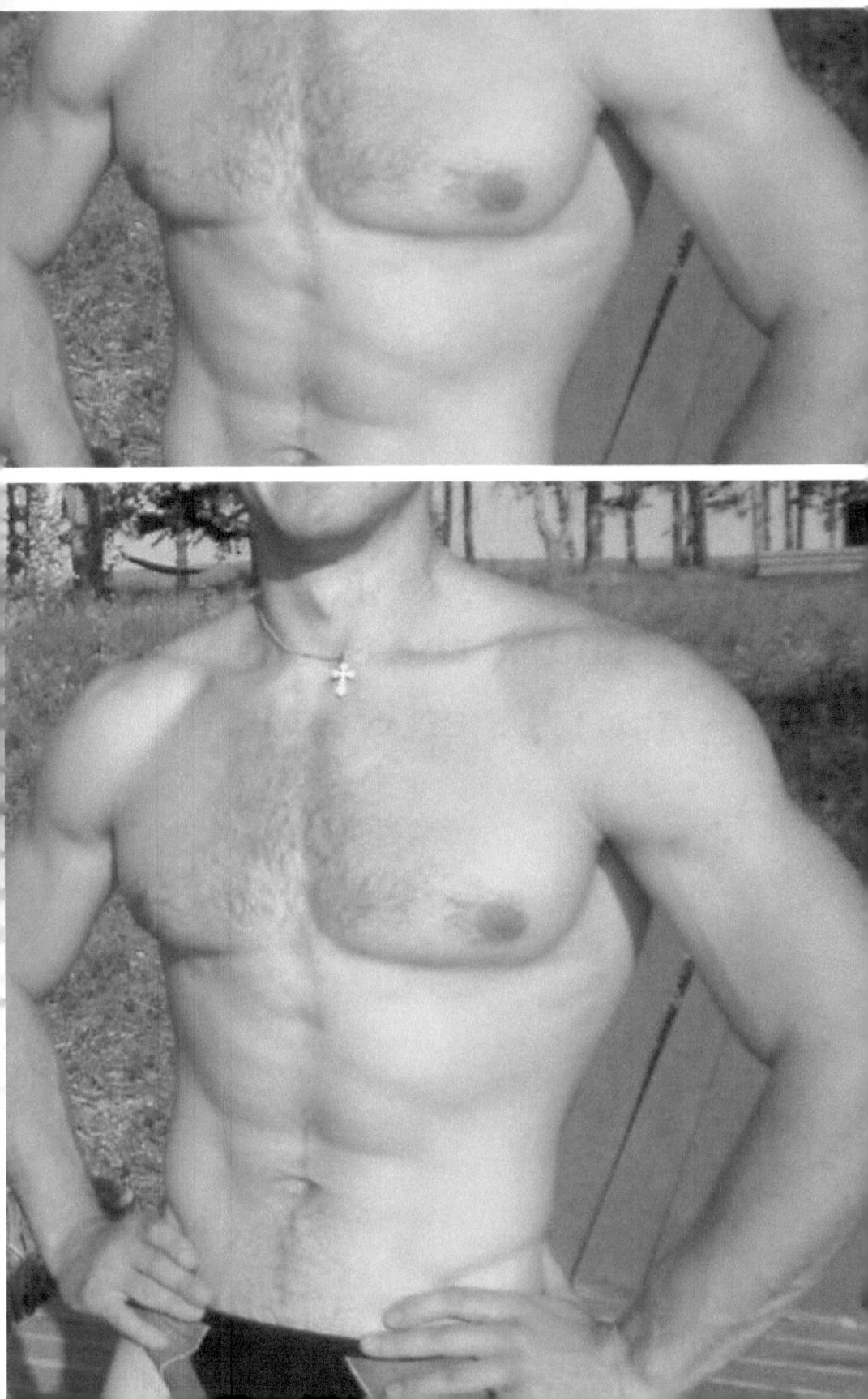

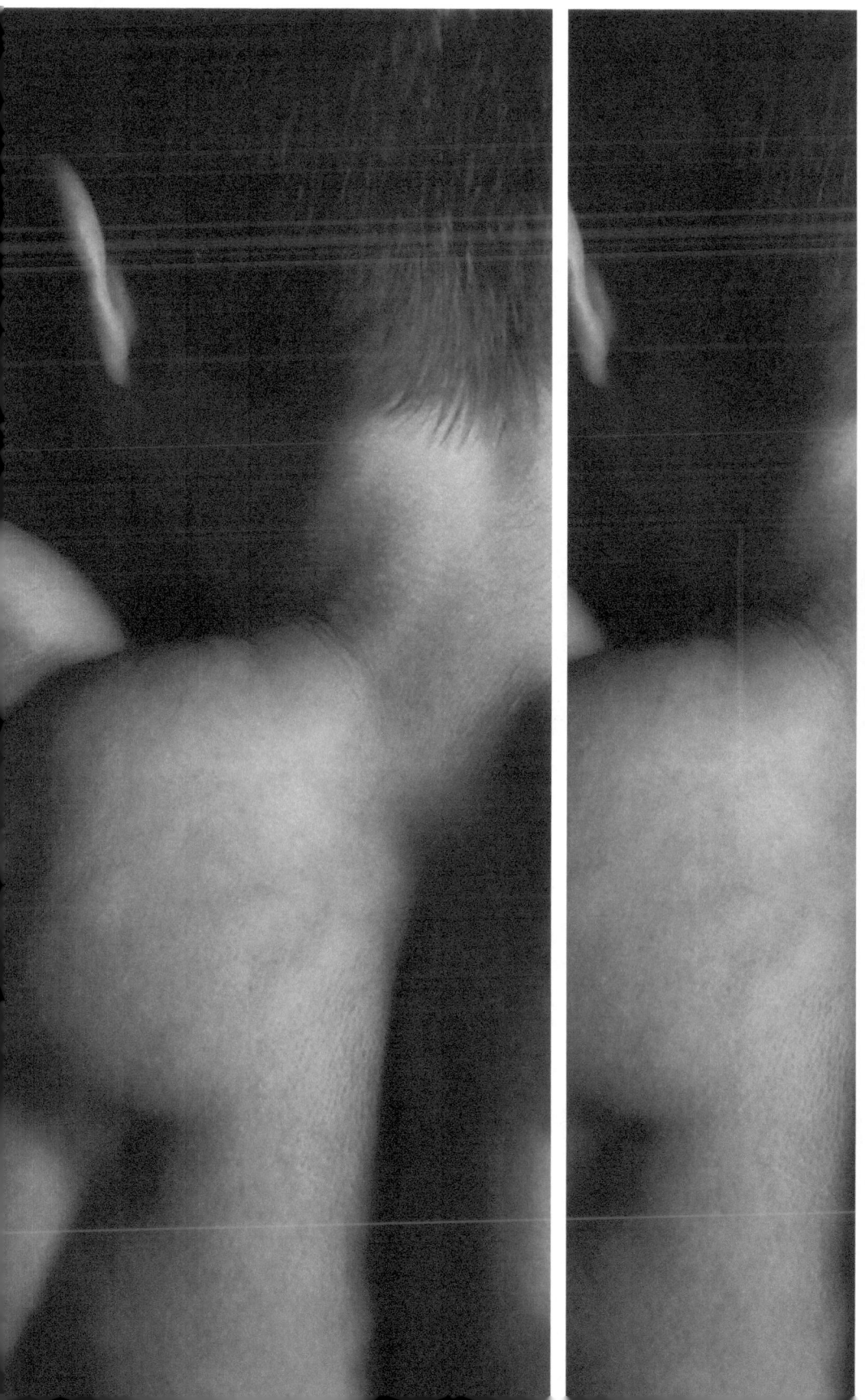

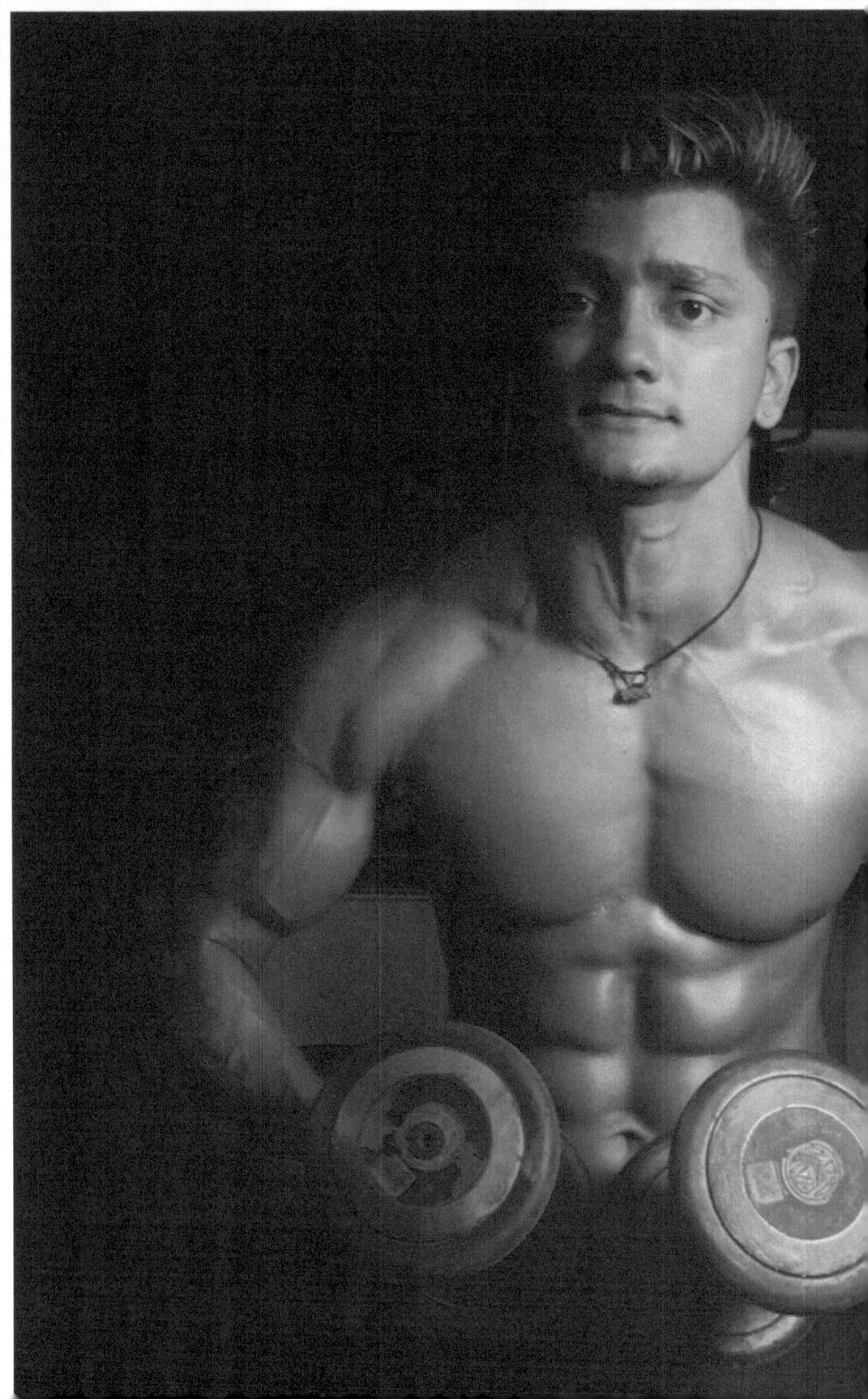

Eighty percent of success is showing up.
Woody Allen

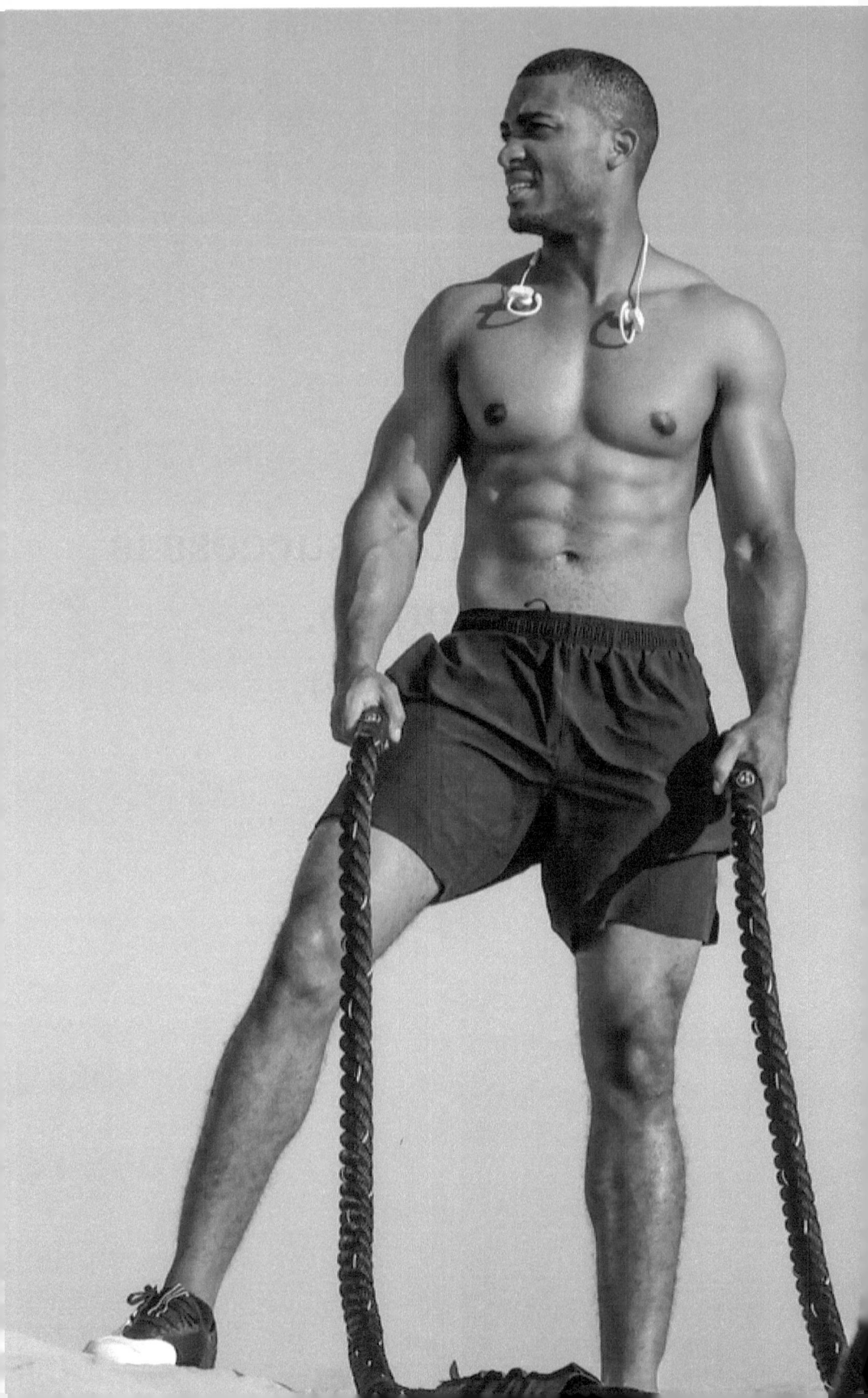

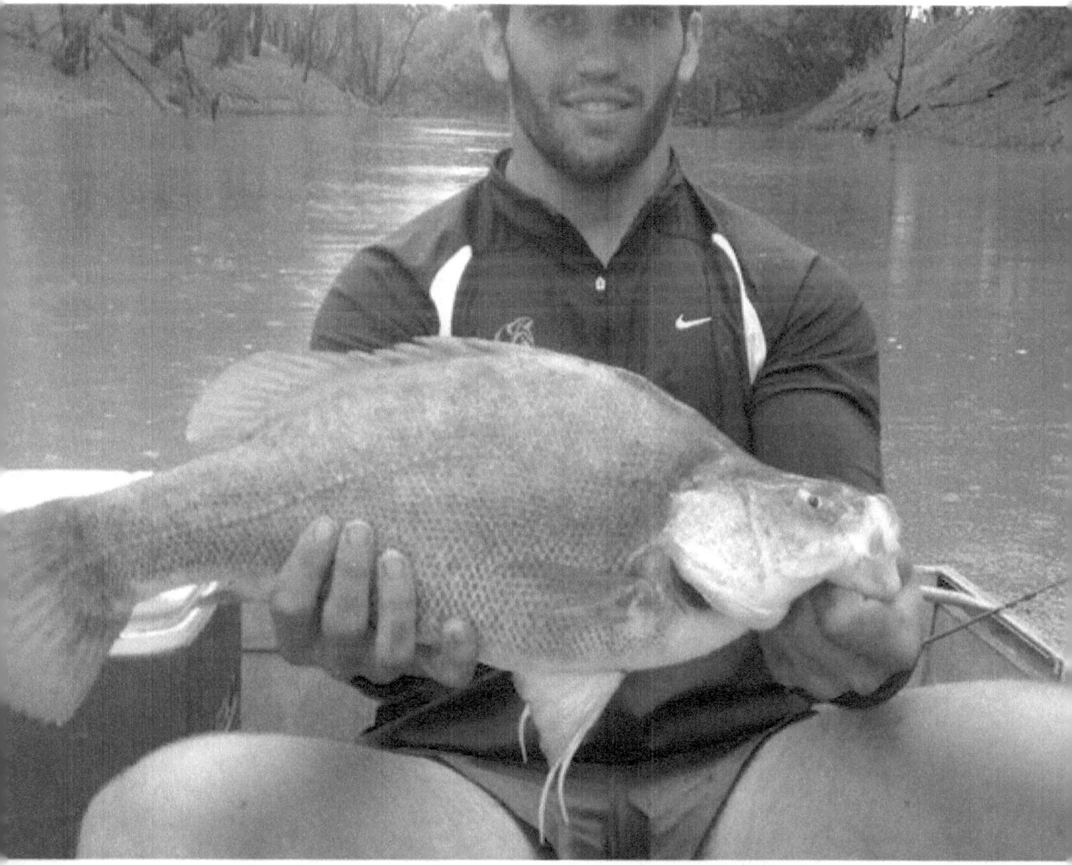

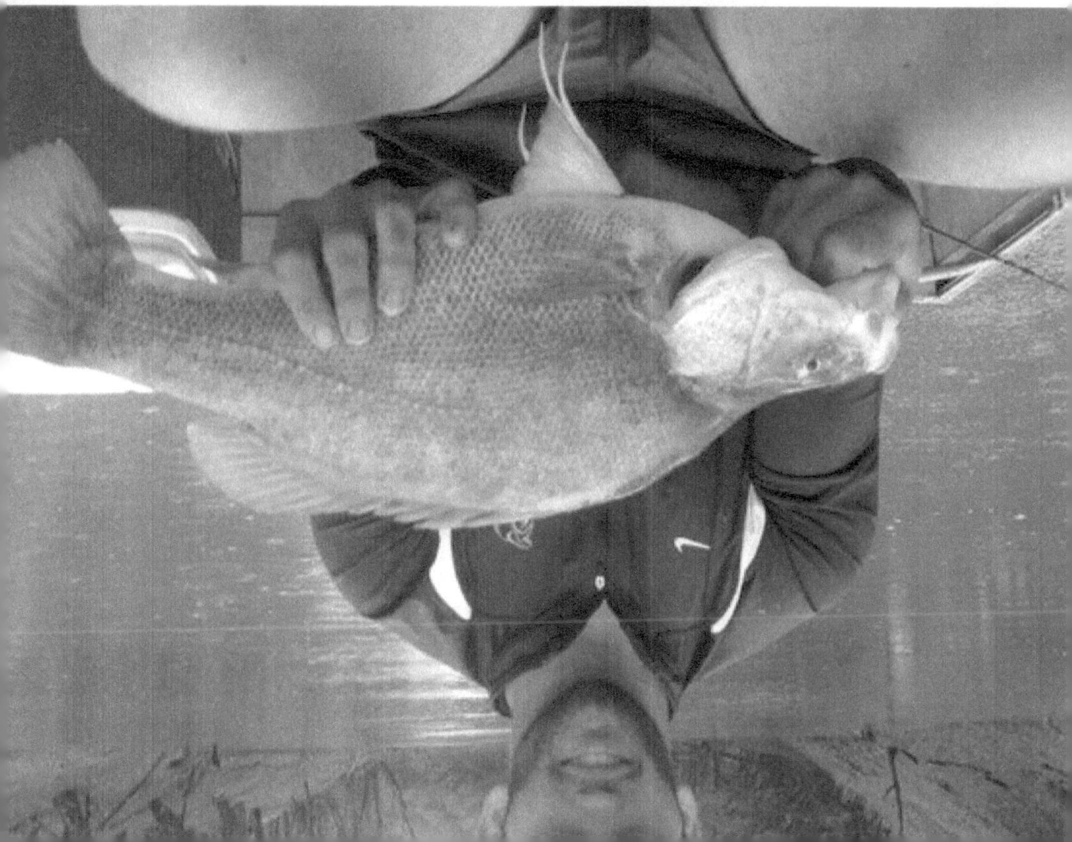

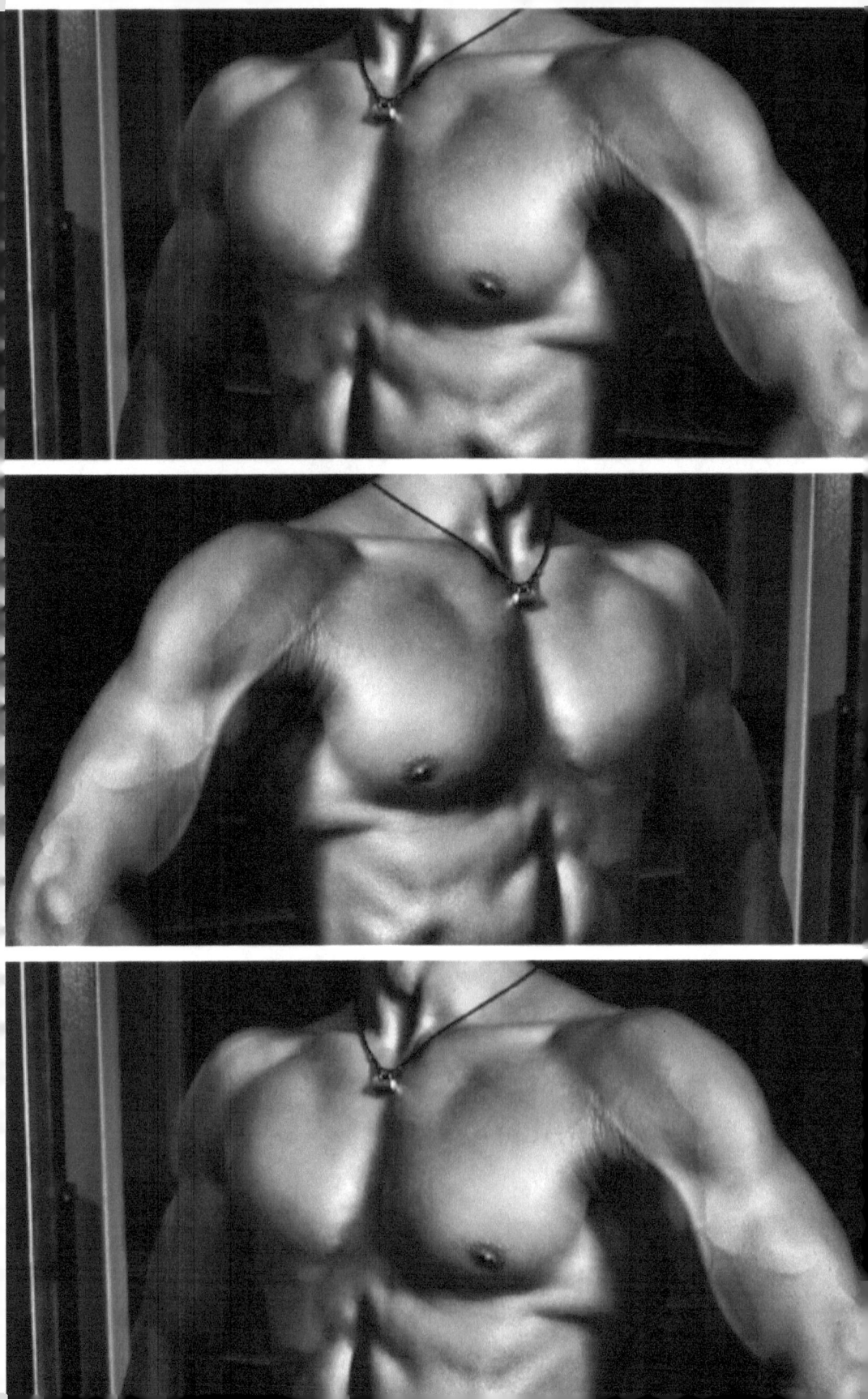

Life isn't about finding yourself. Life is about creating yourself.
George Bernard Shaw

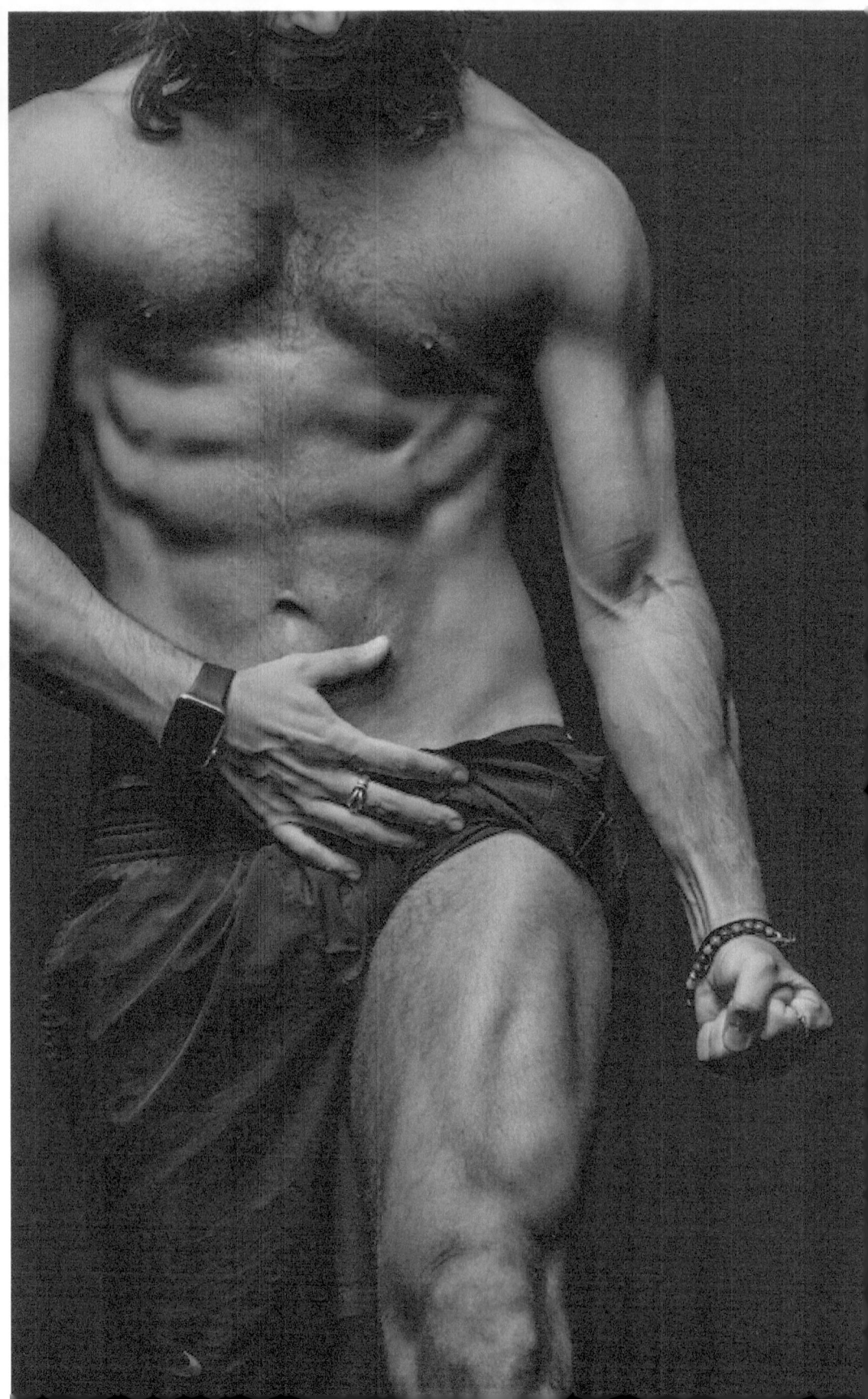

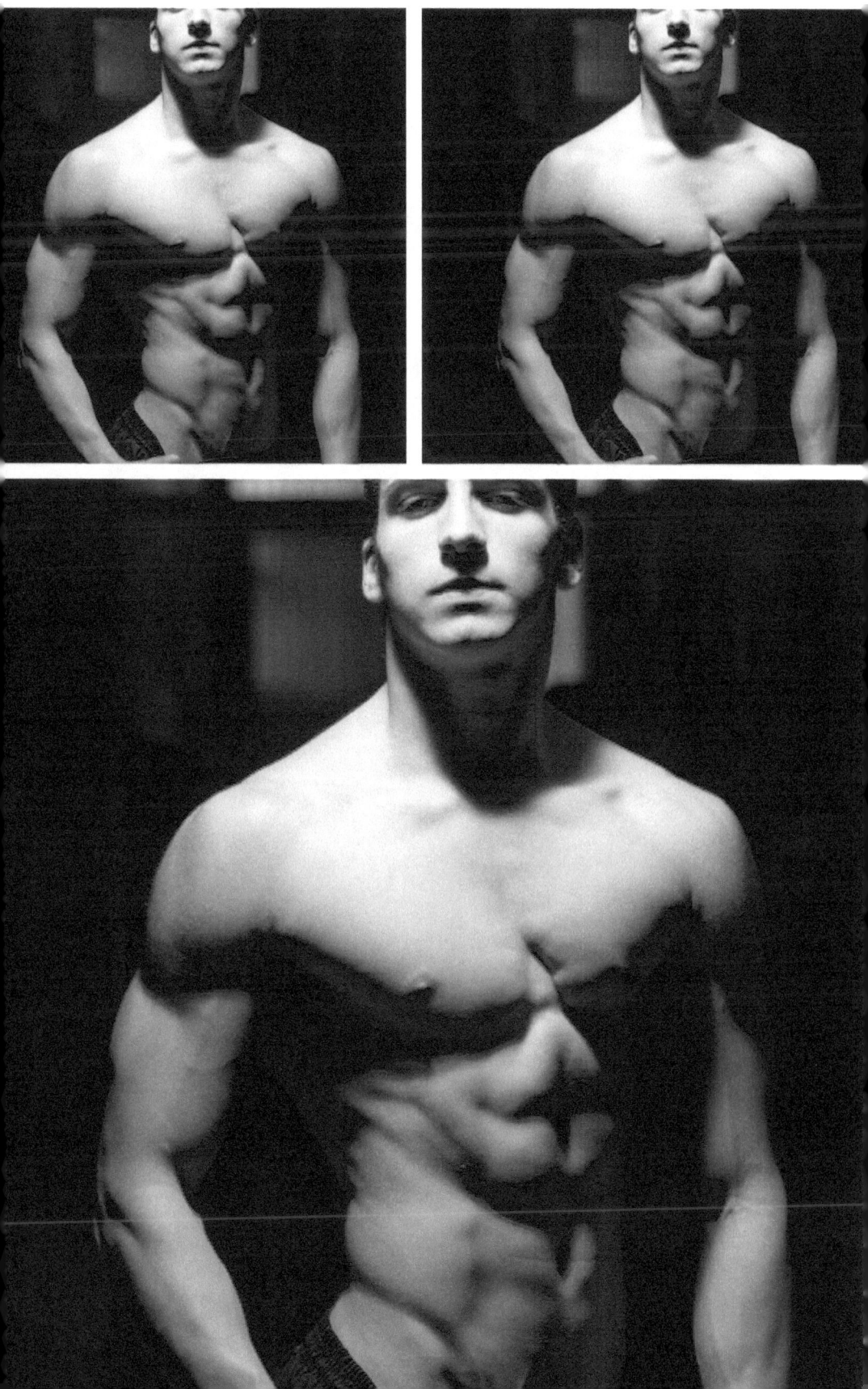

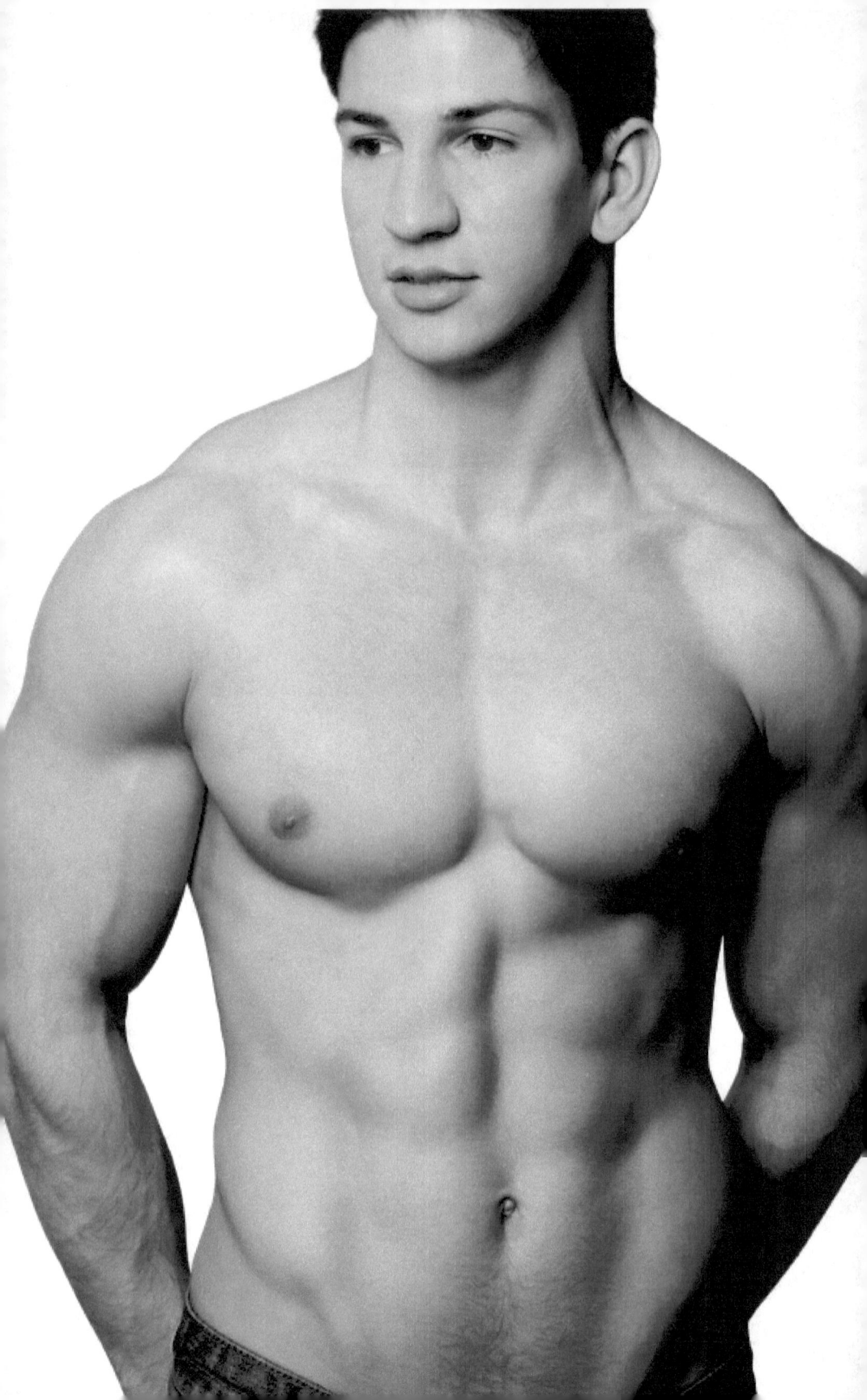

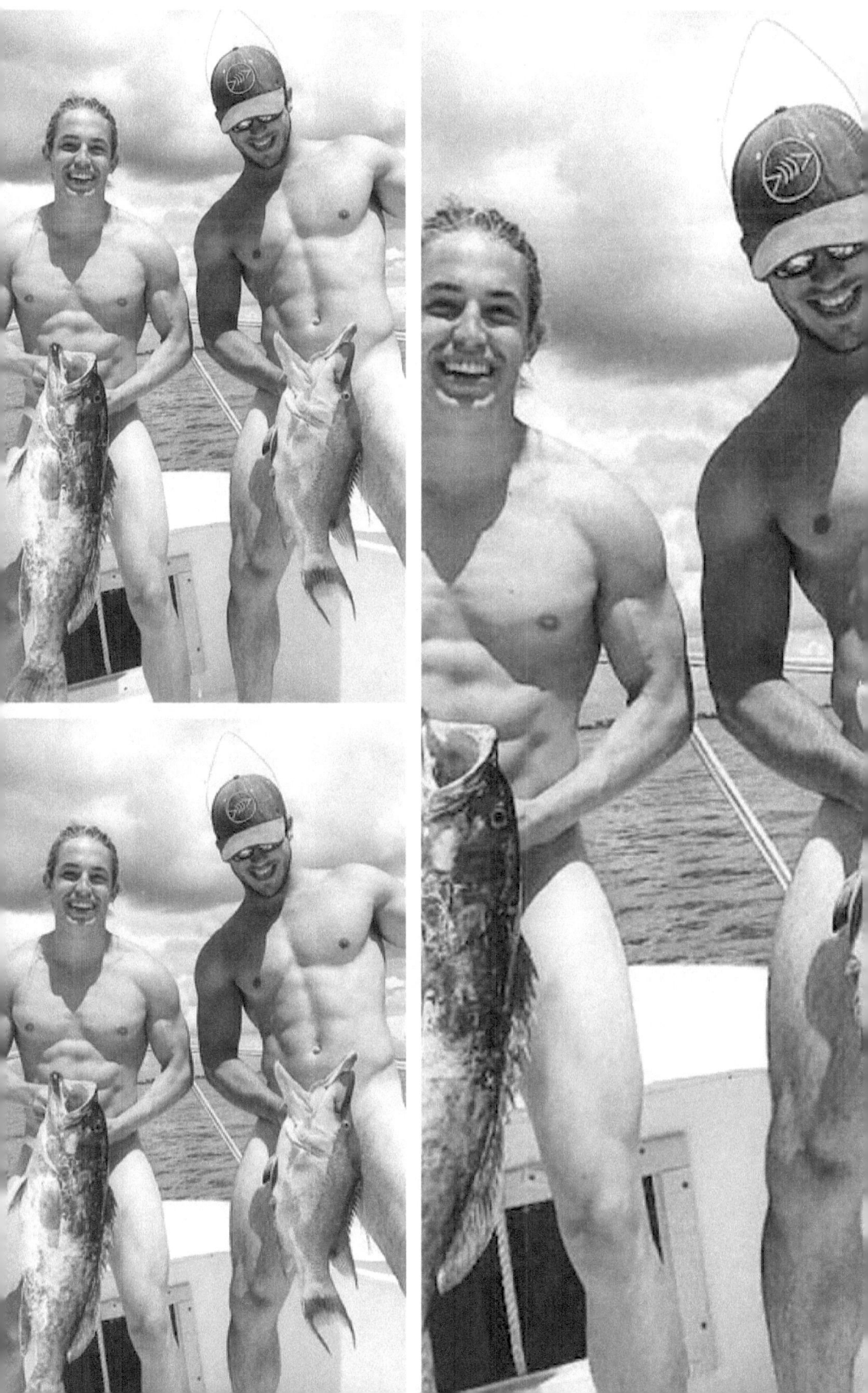

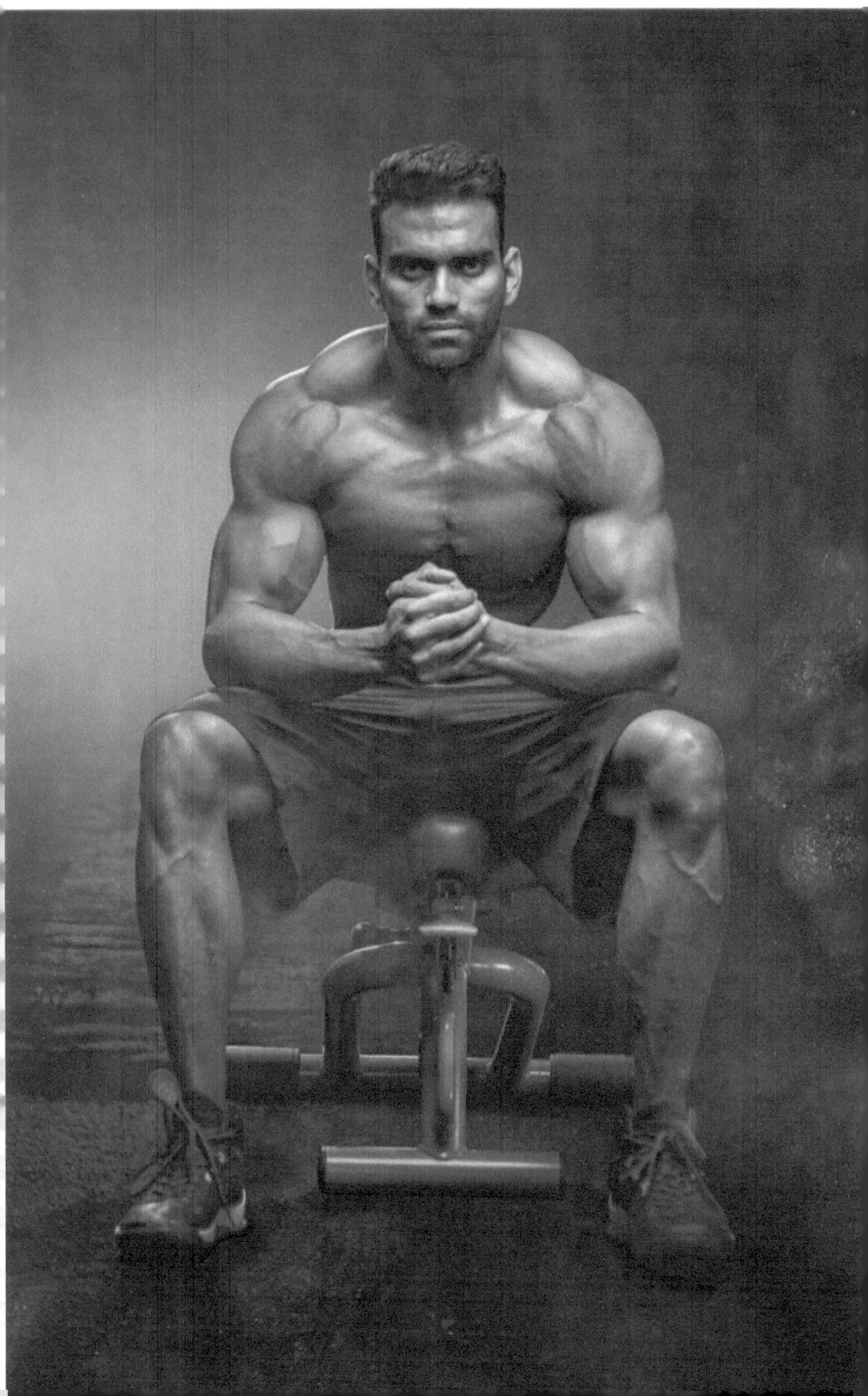

Doing something for yourself like running, and using it to test yourself, will only make you feel better about your career or your family role.
Joan Benoit

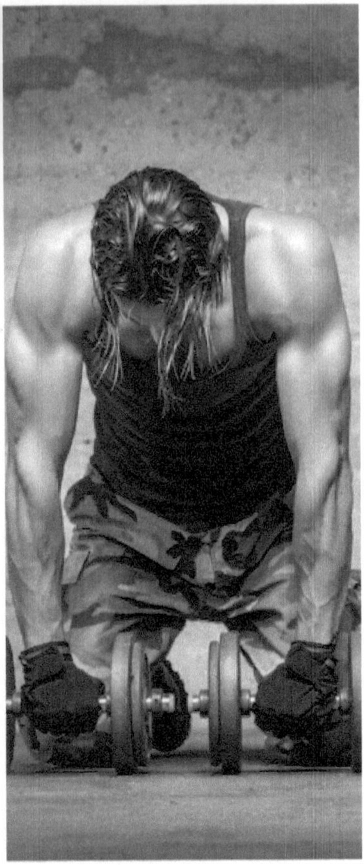

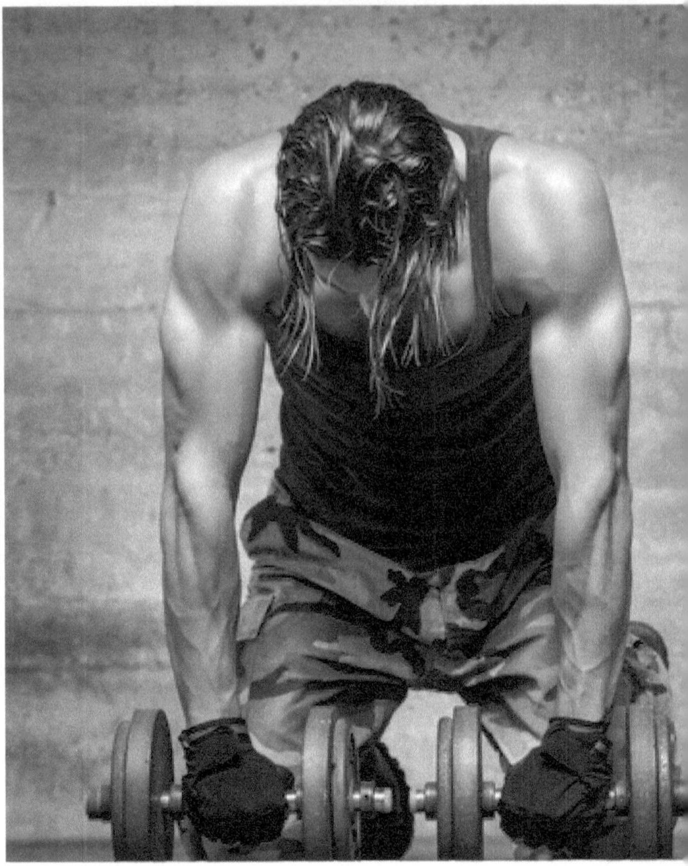

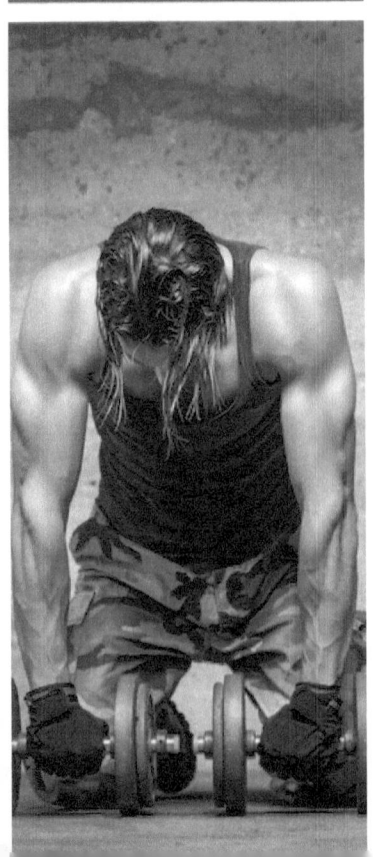
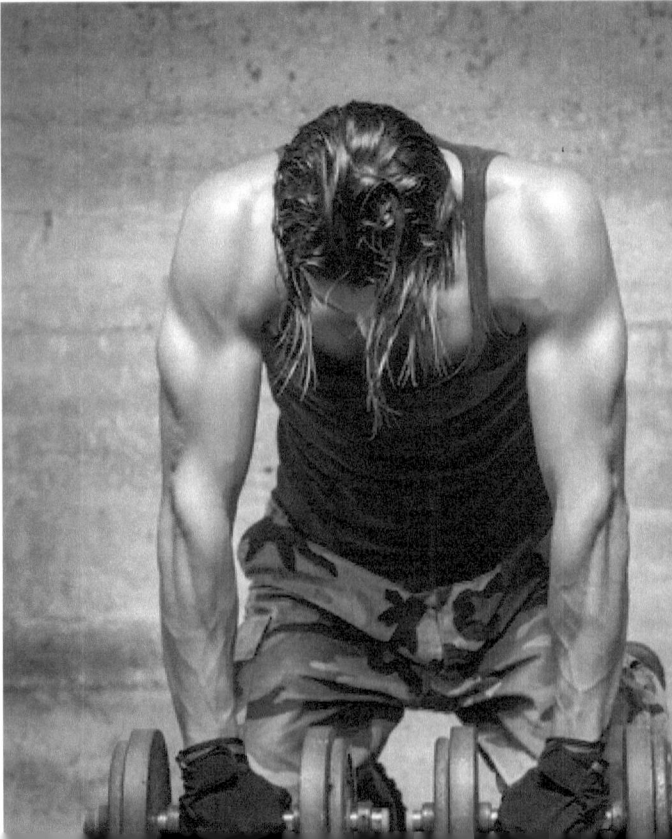

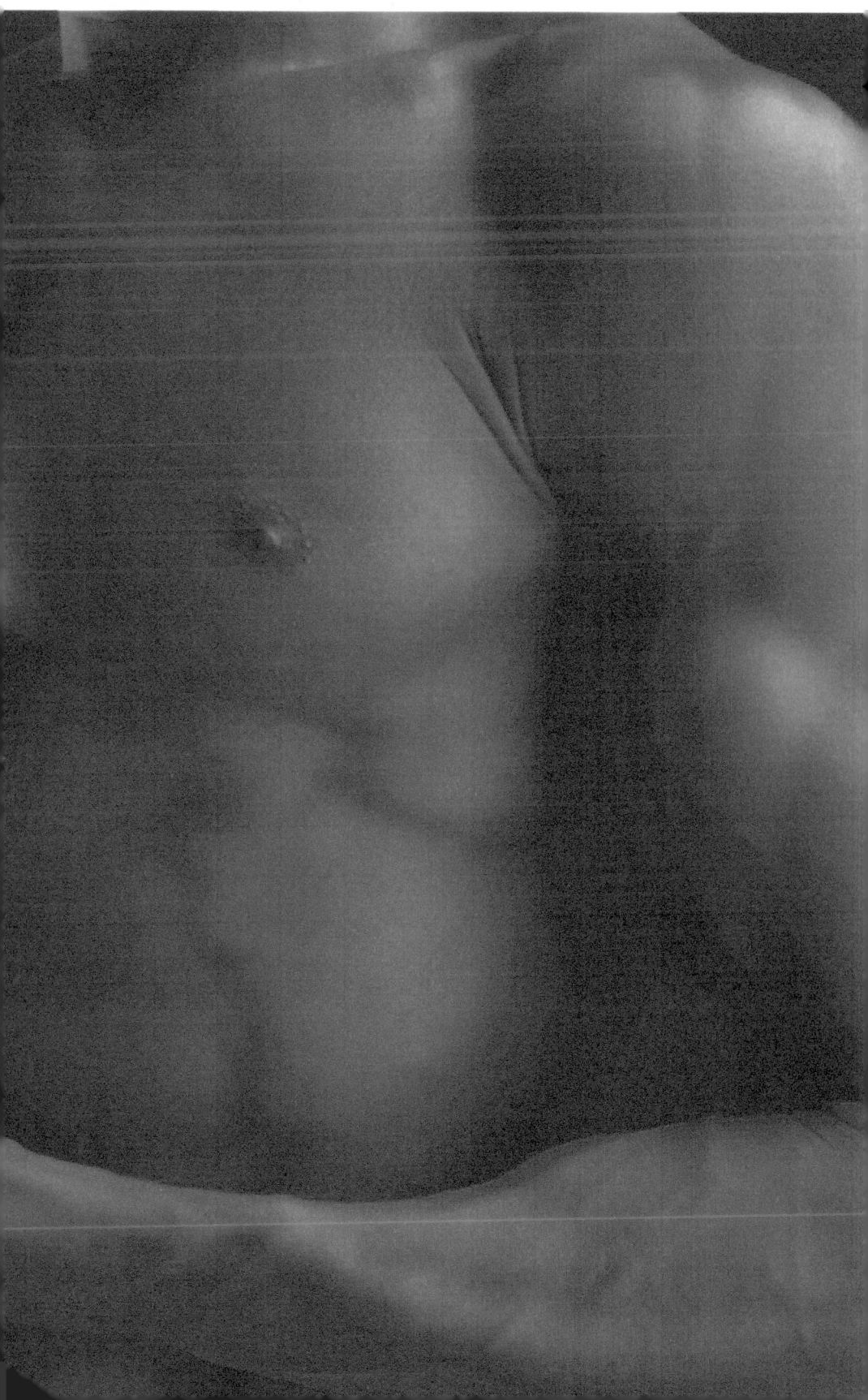

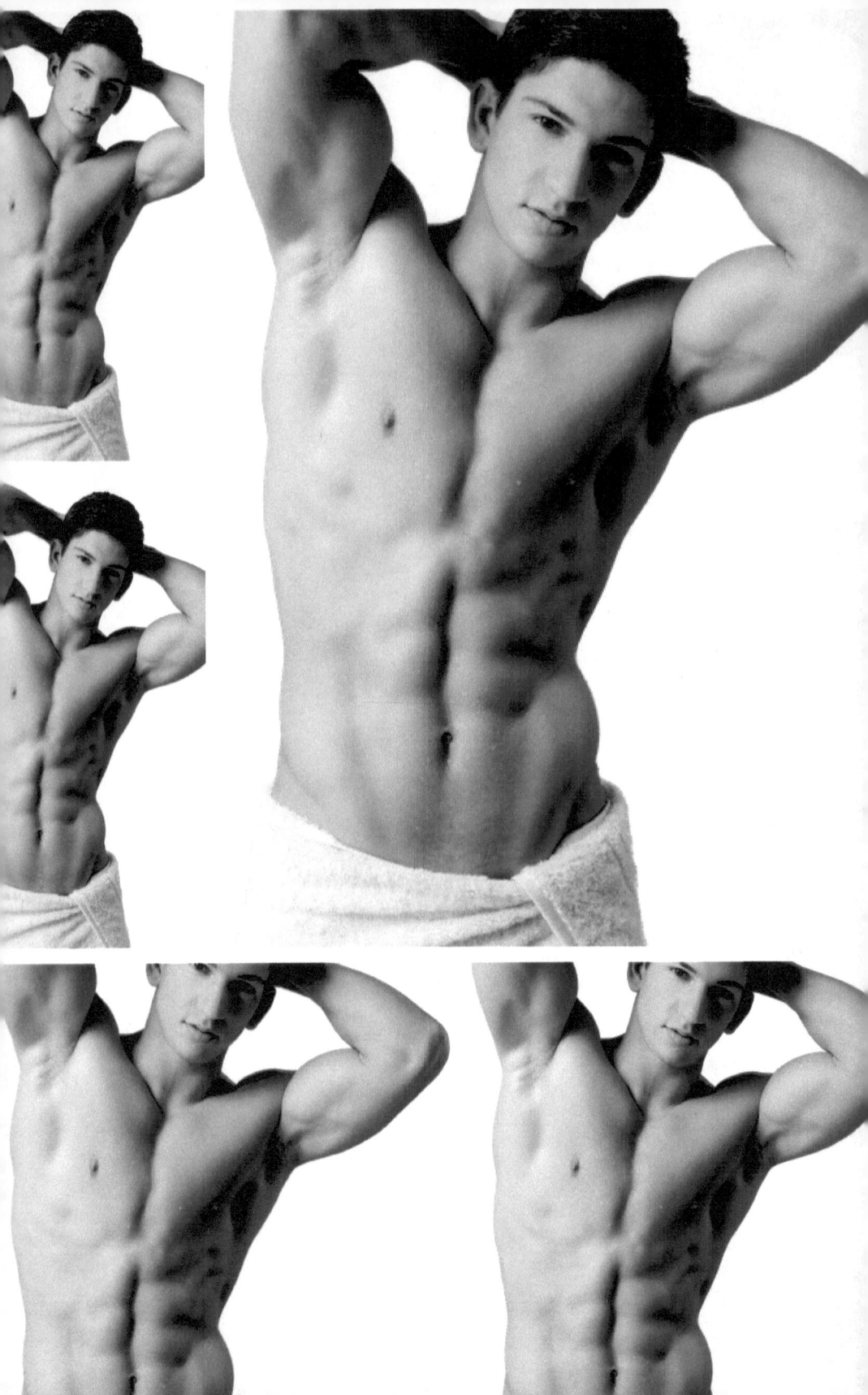

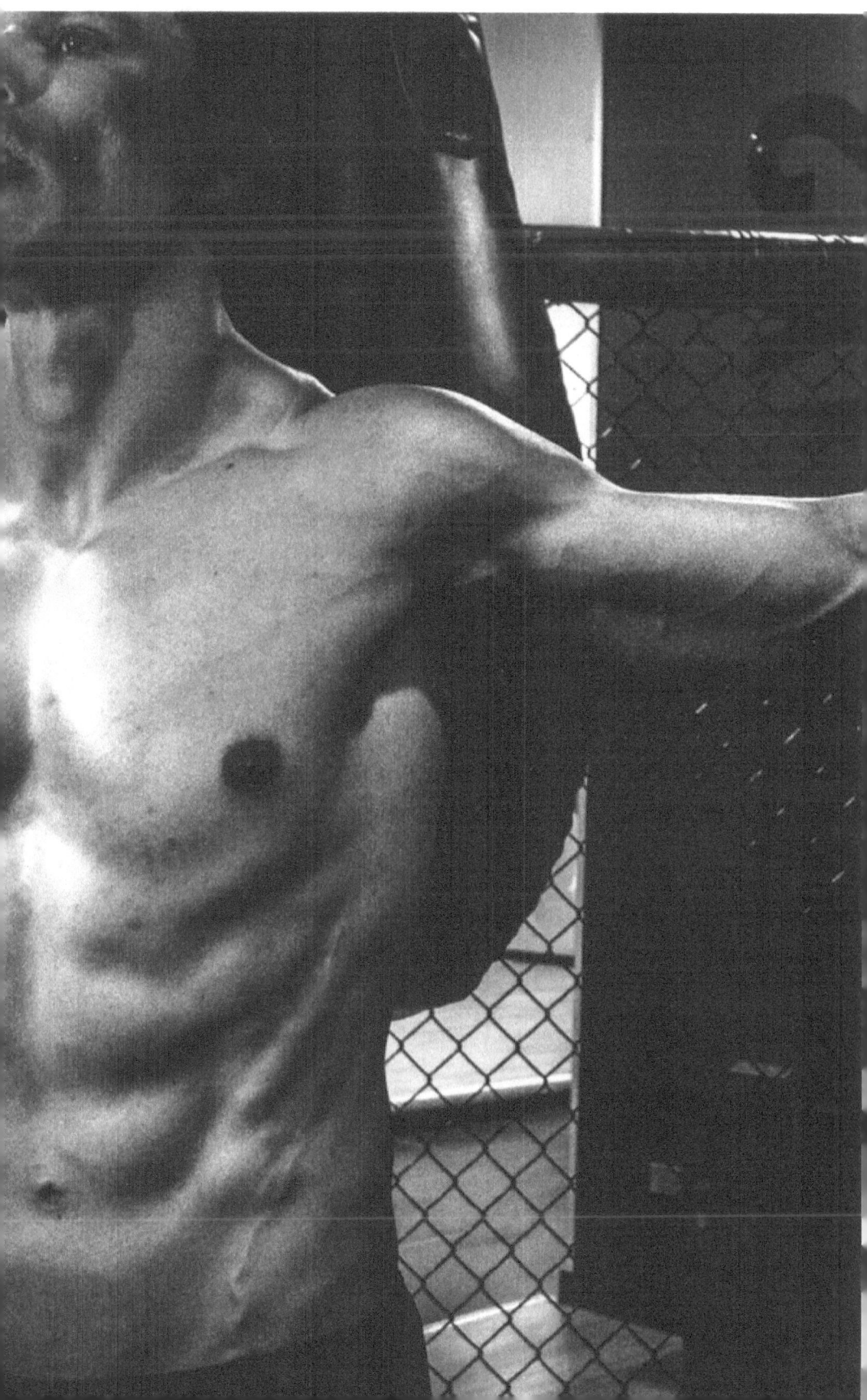

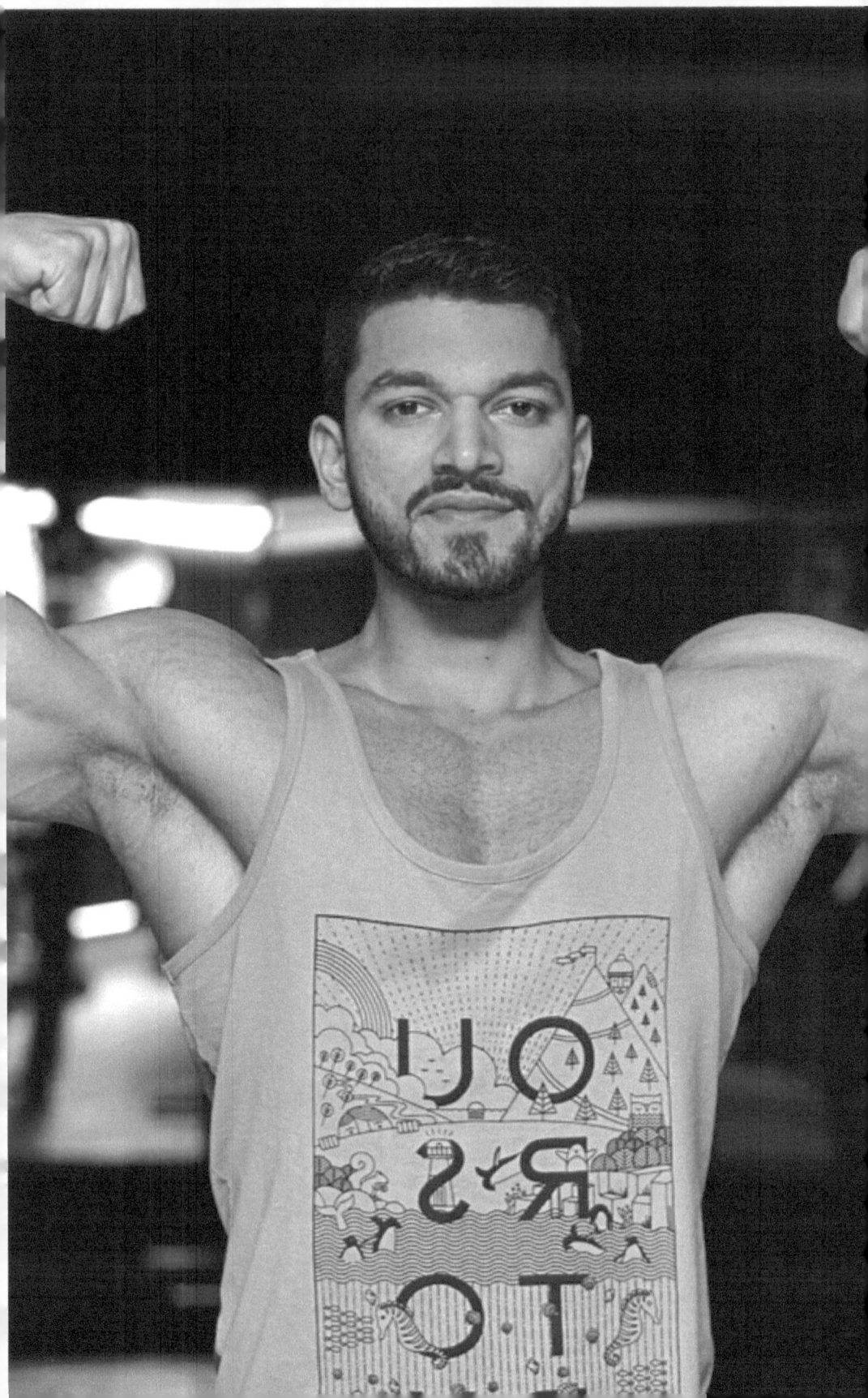

Take care of your body. It's the only place you have to live.
Jim Rohn

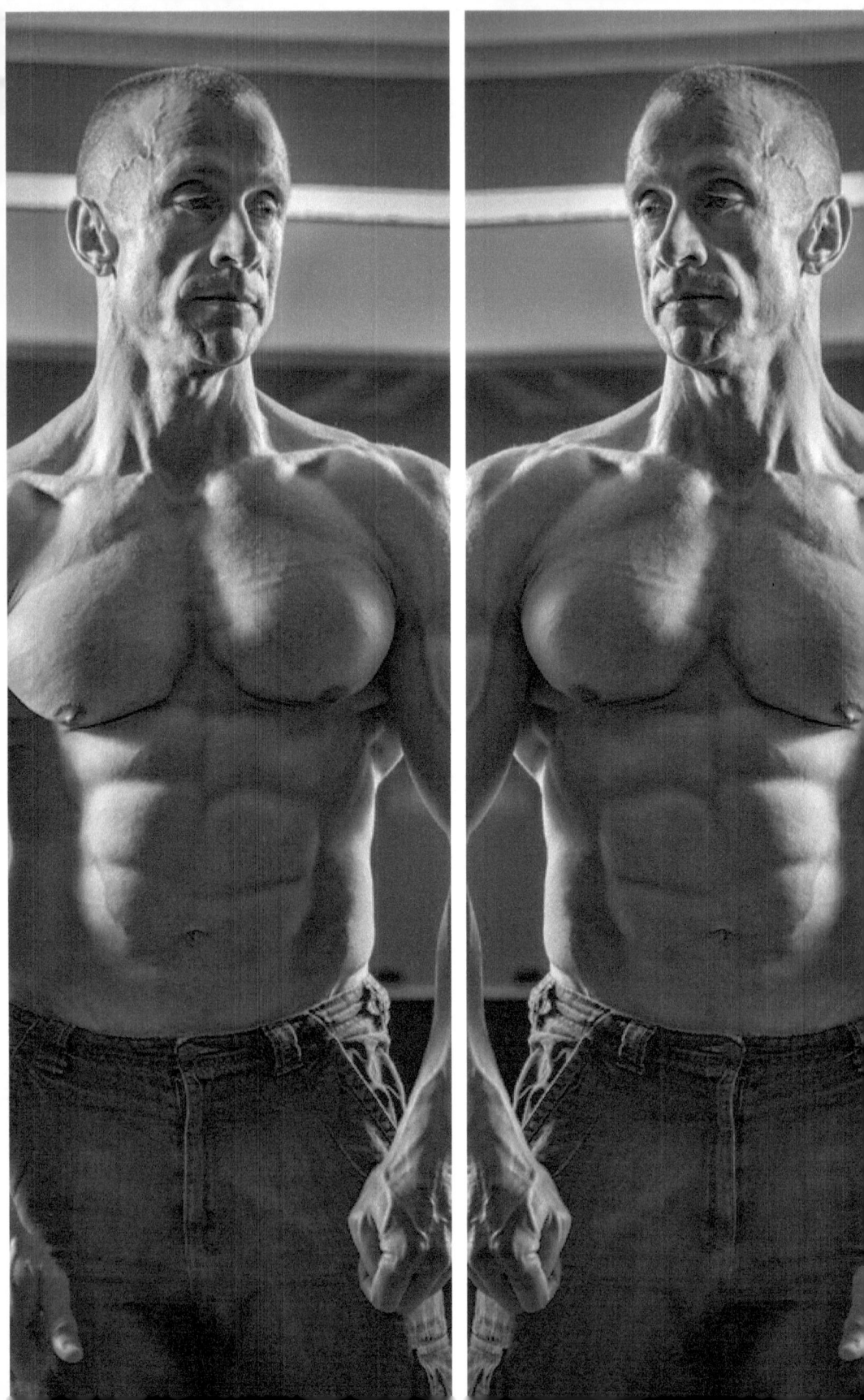

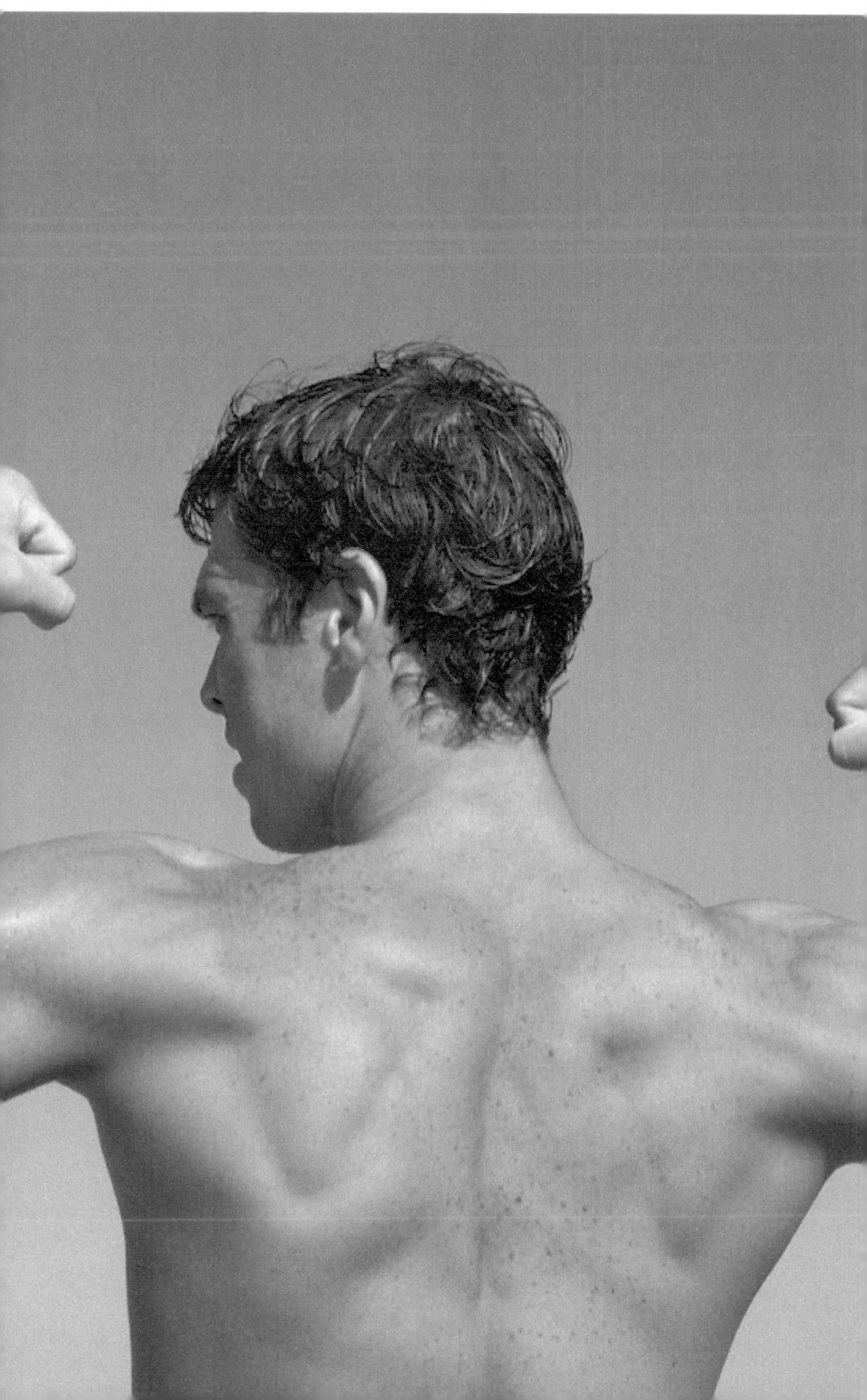

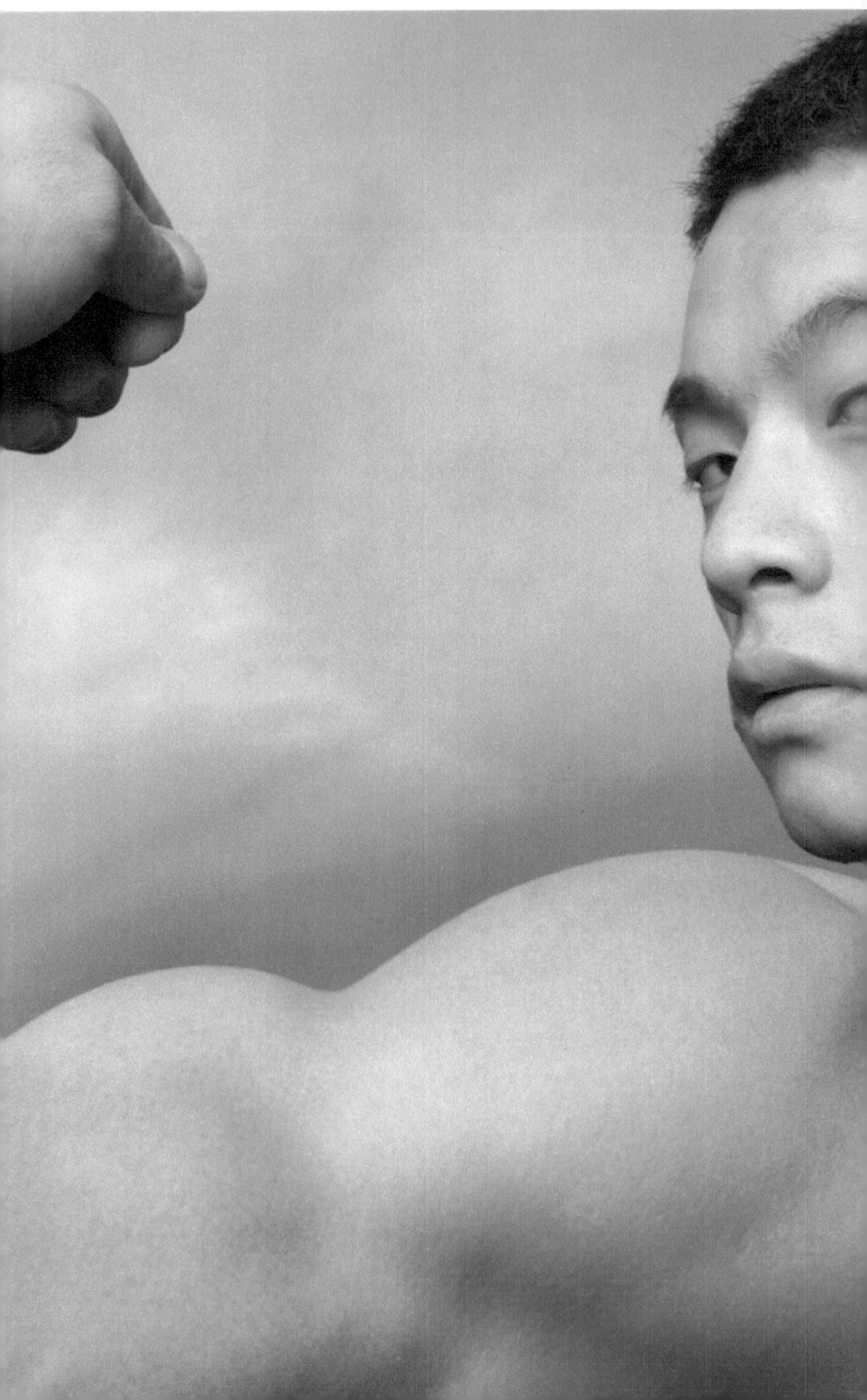

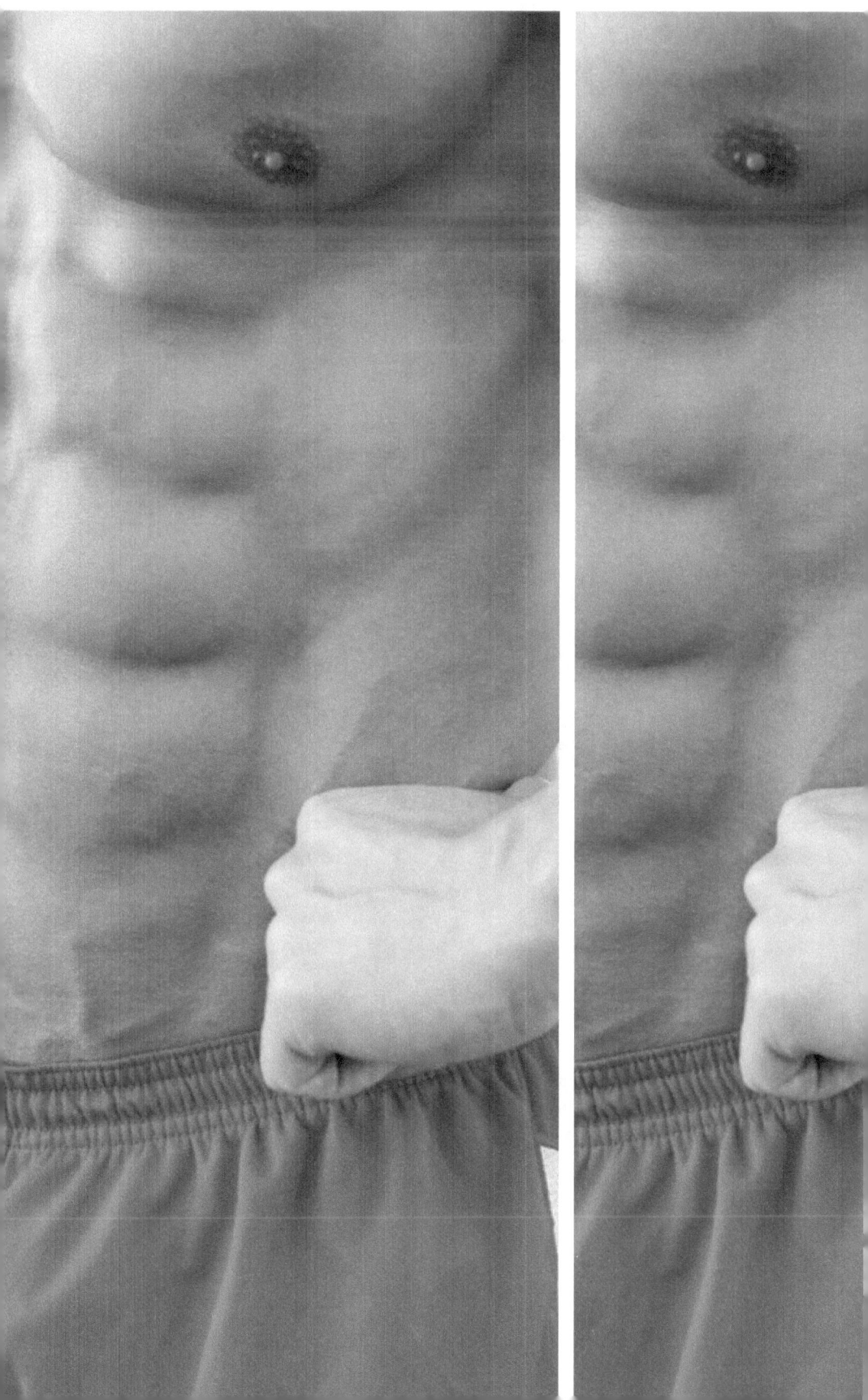

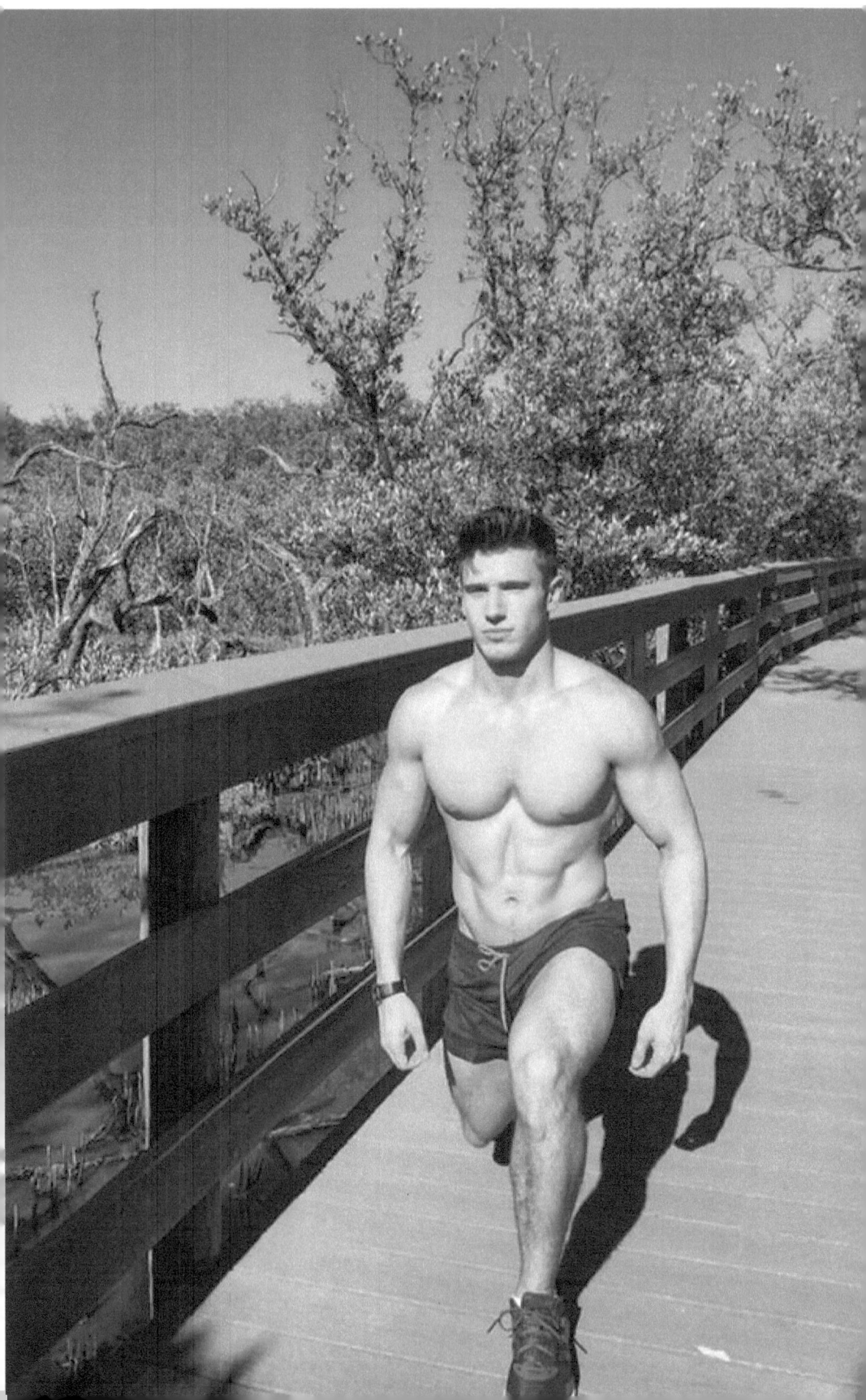

Strength does not come from physical capacity. It comes from an indomitable will.
Mahatma Gandhi

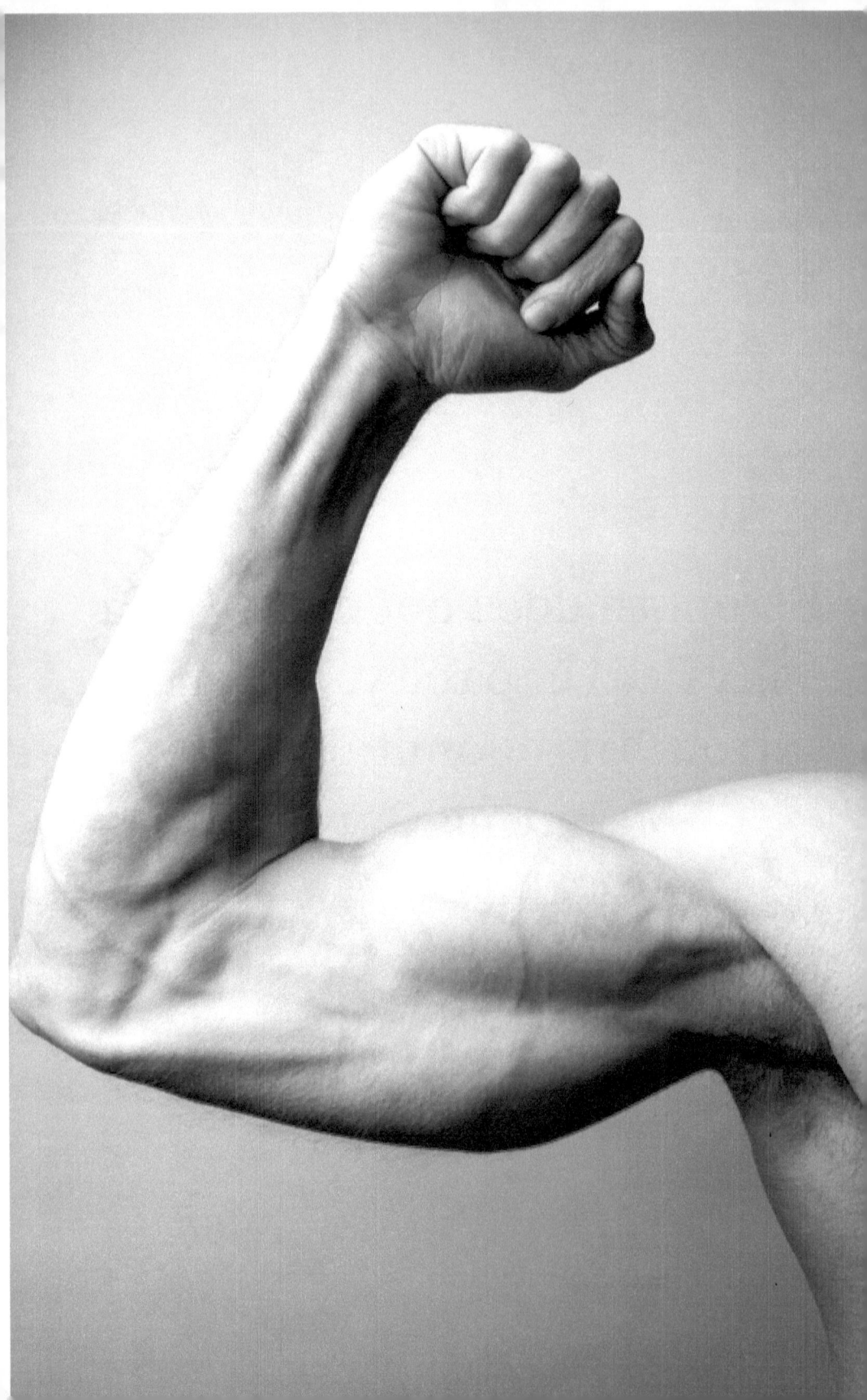

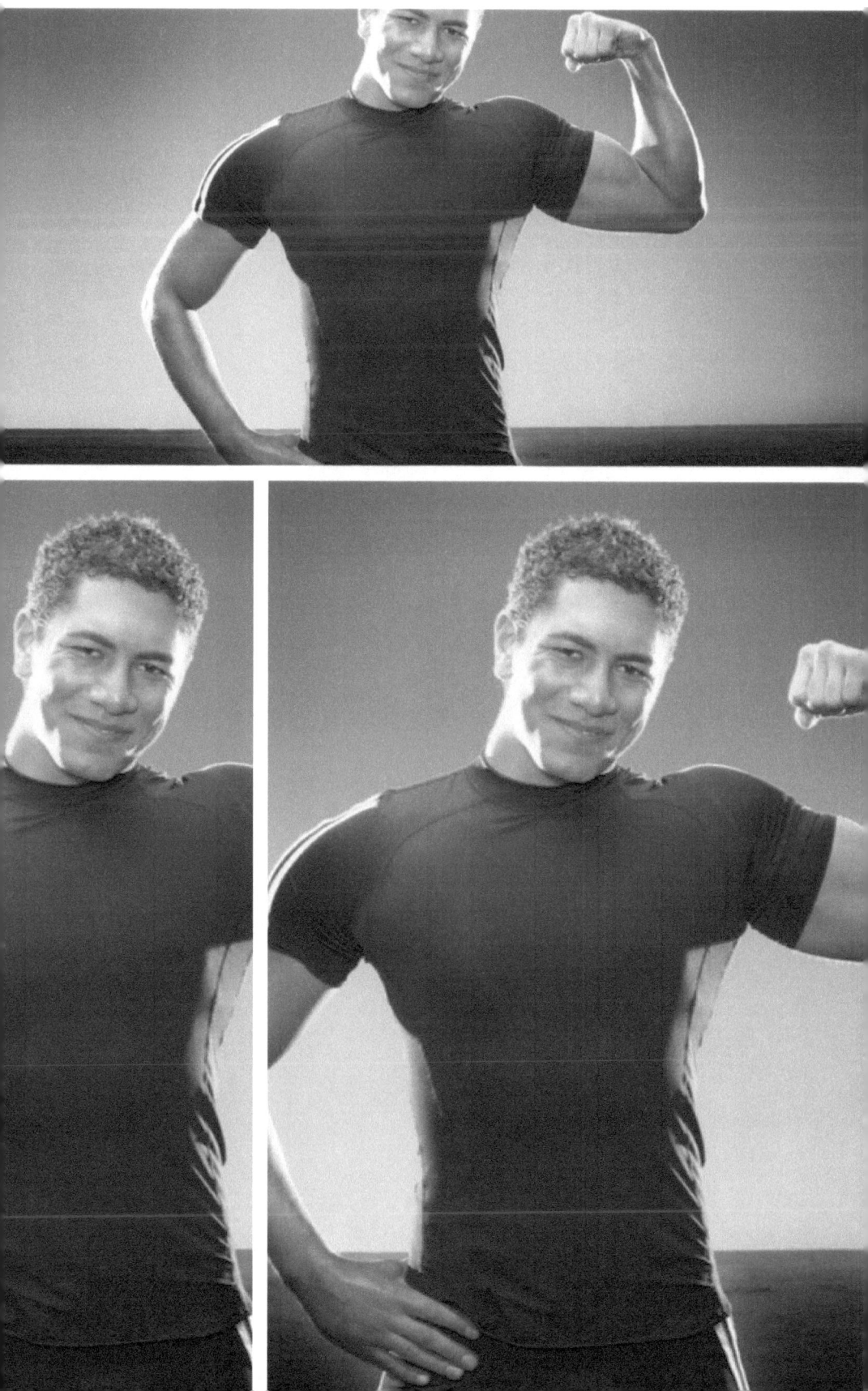

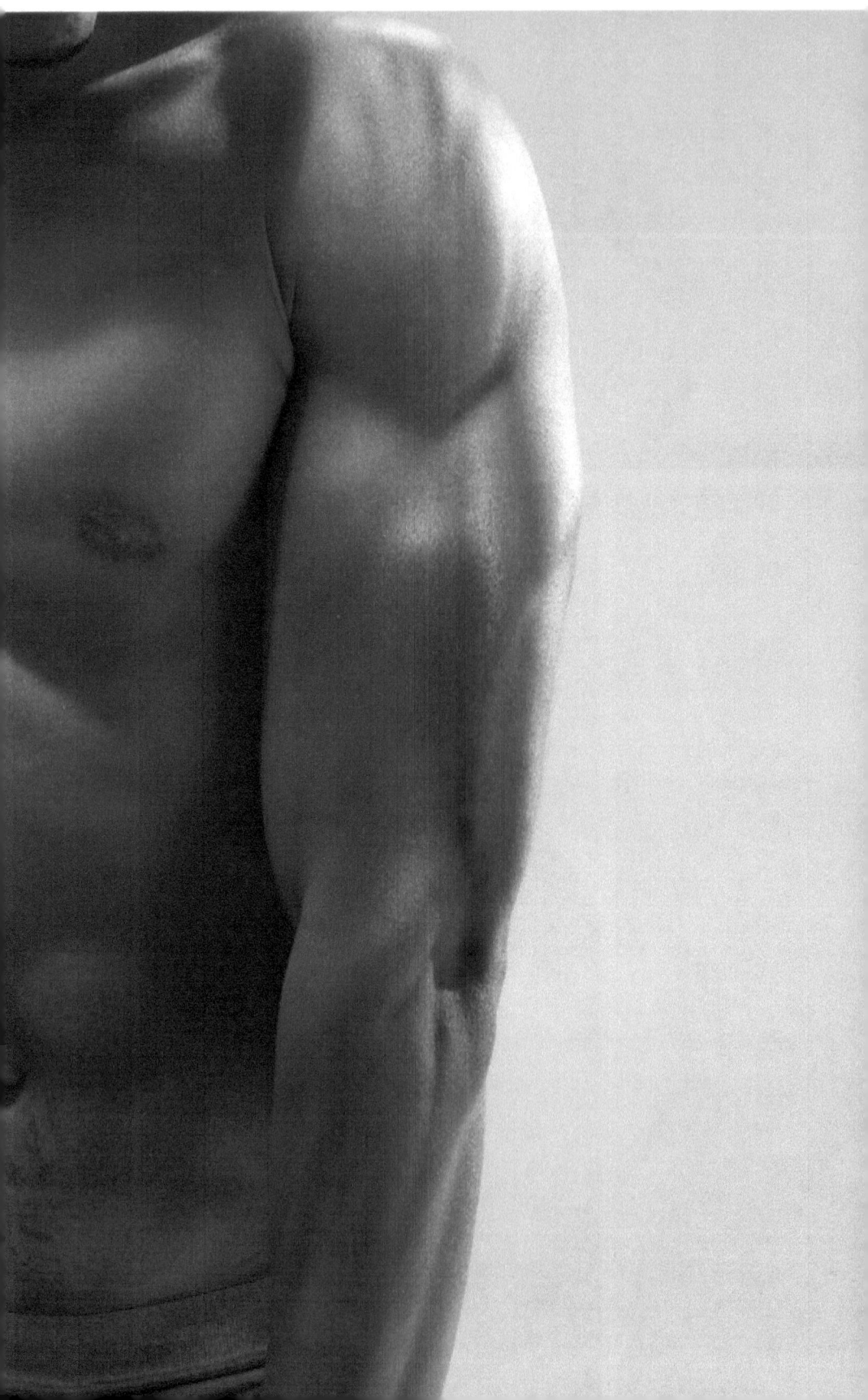

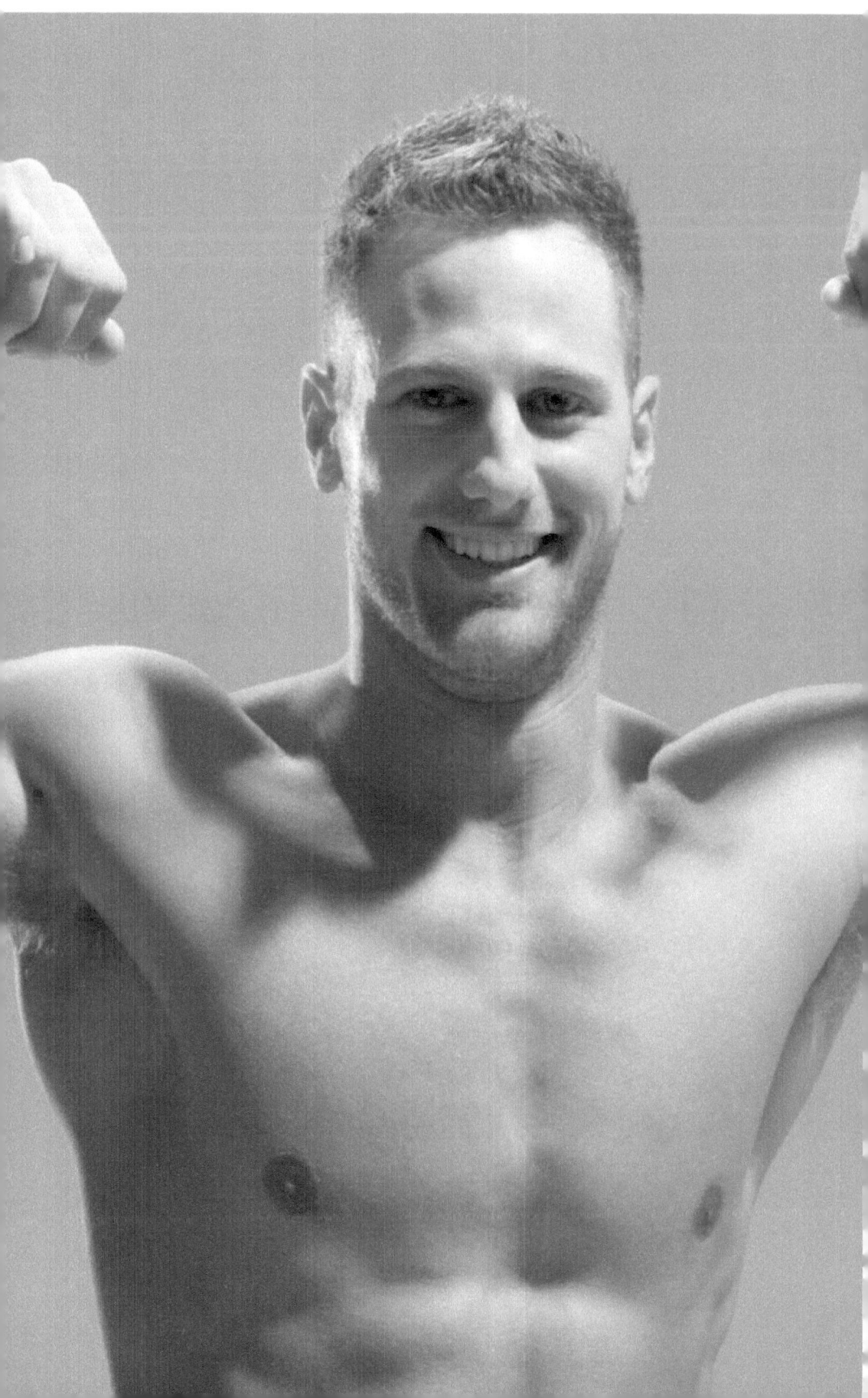

Living a healthy lifestyle
will only deprive you of poor
health, lethargy, and fat.
Jill Johnson

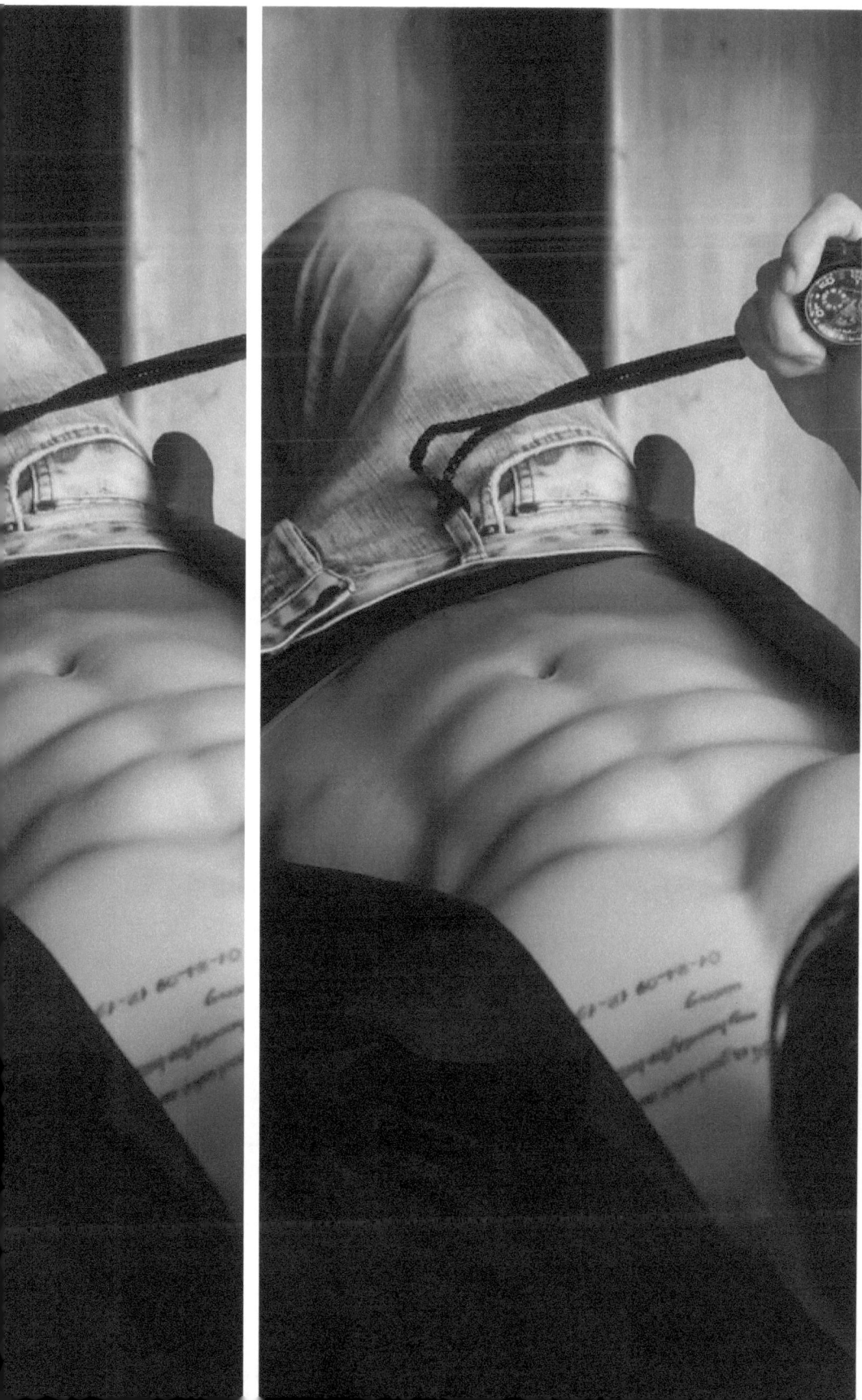

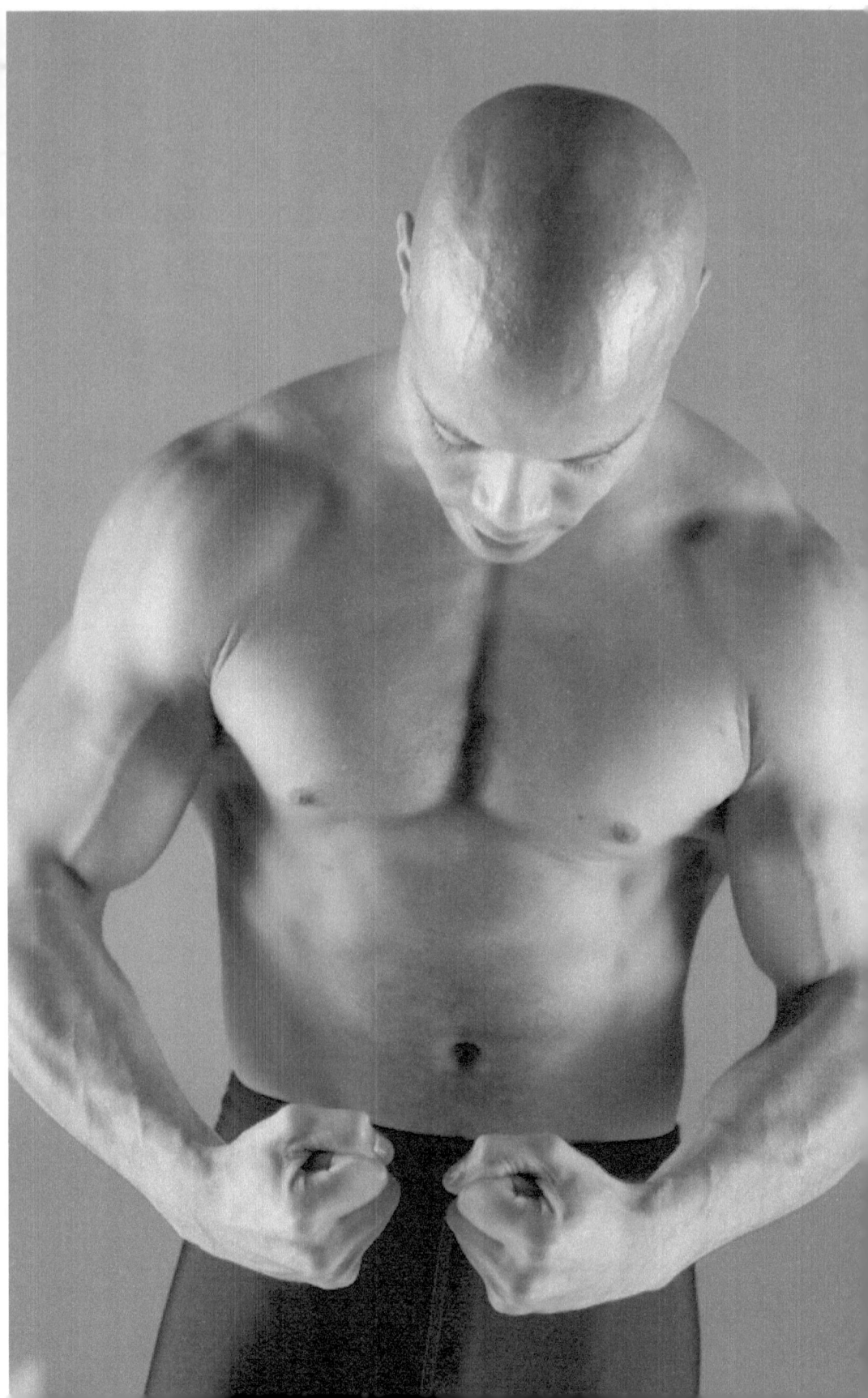

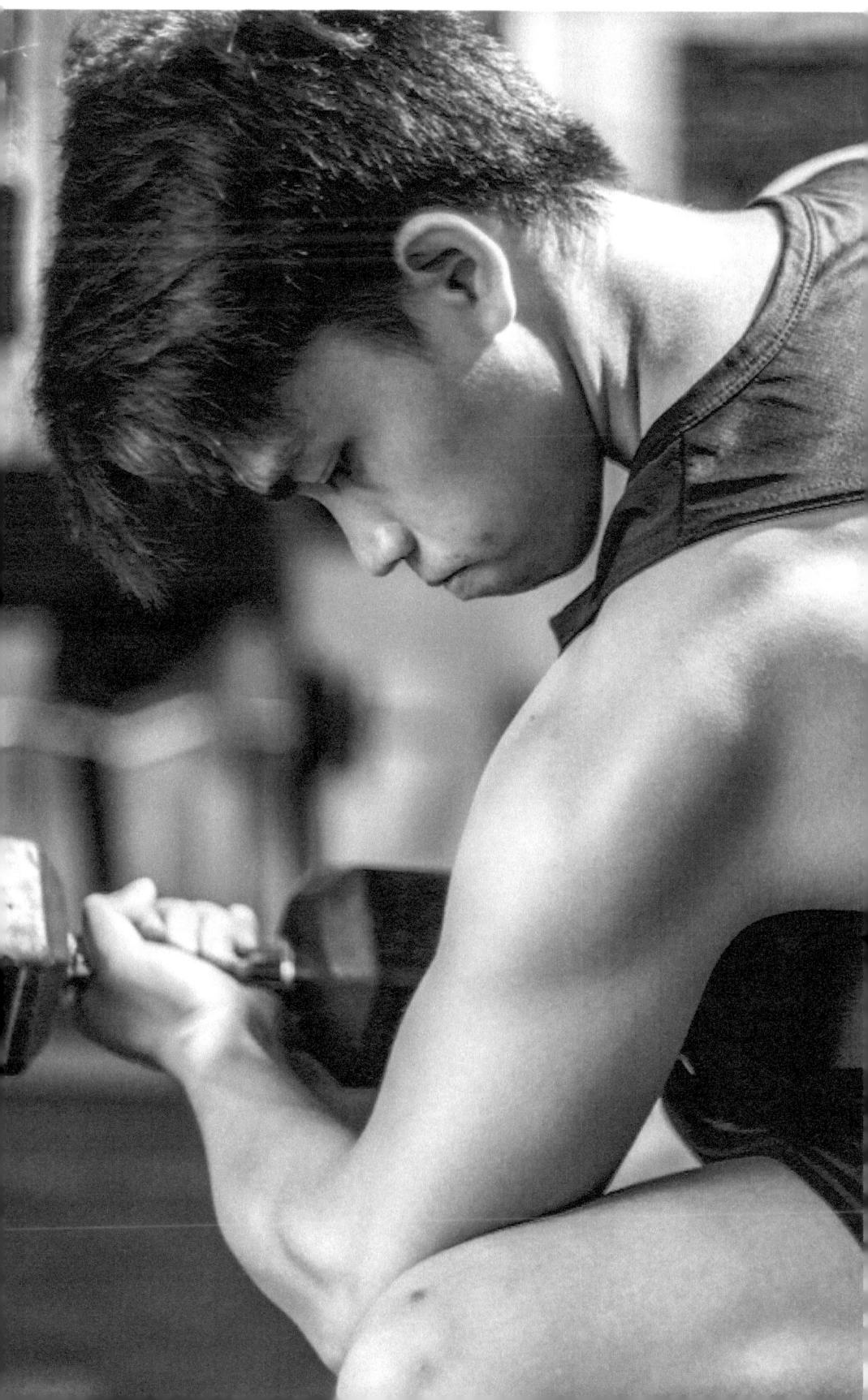

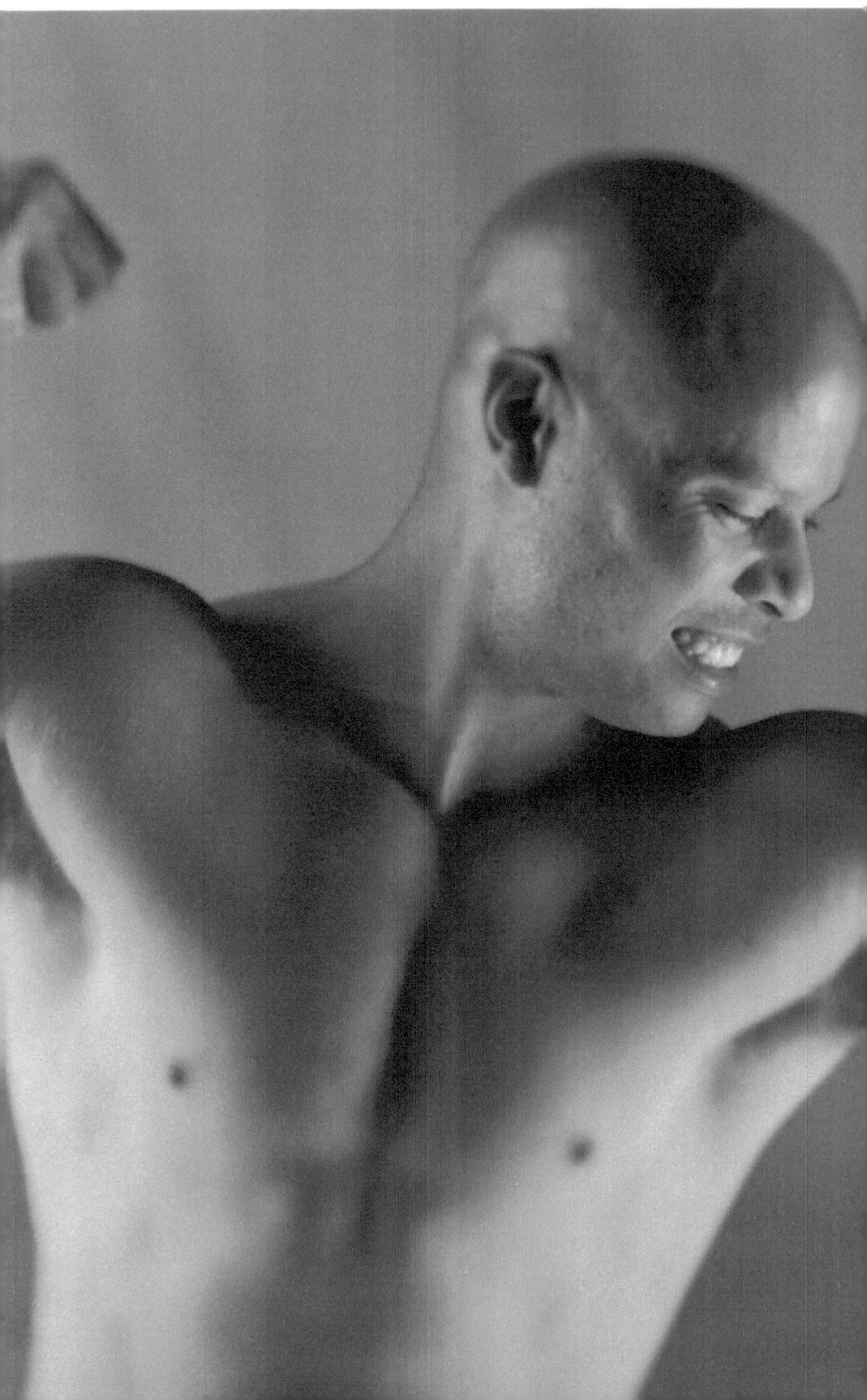

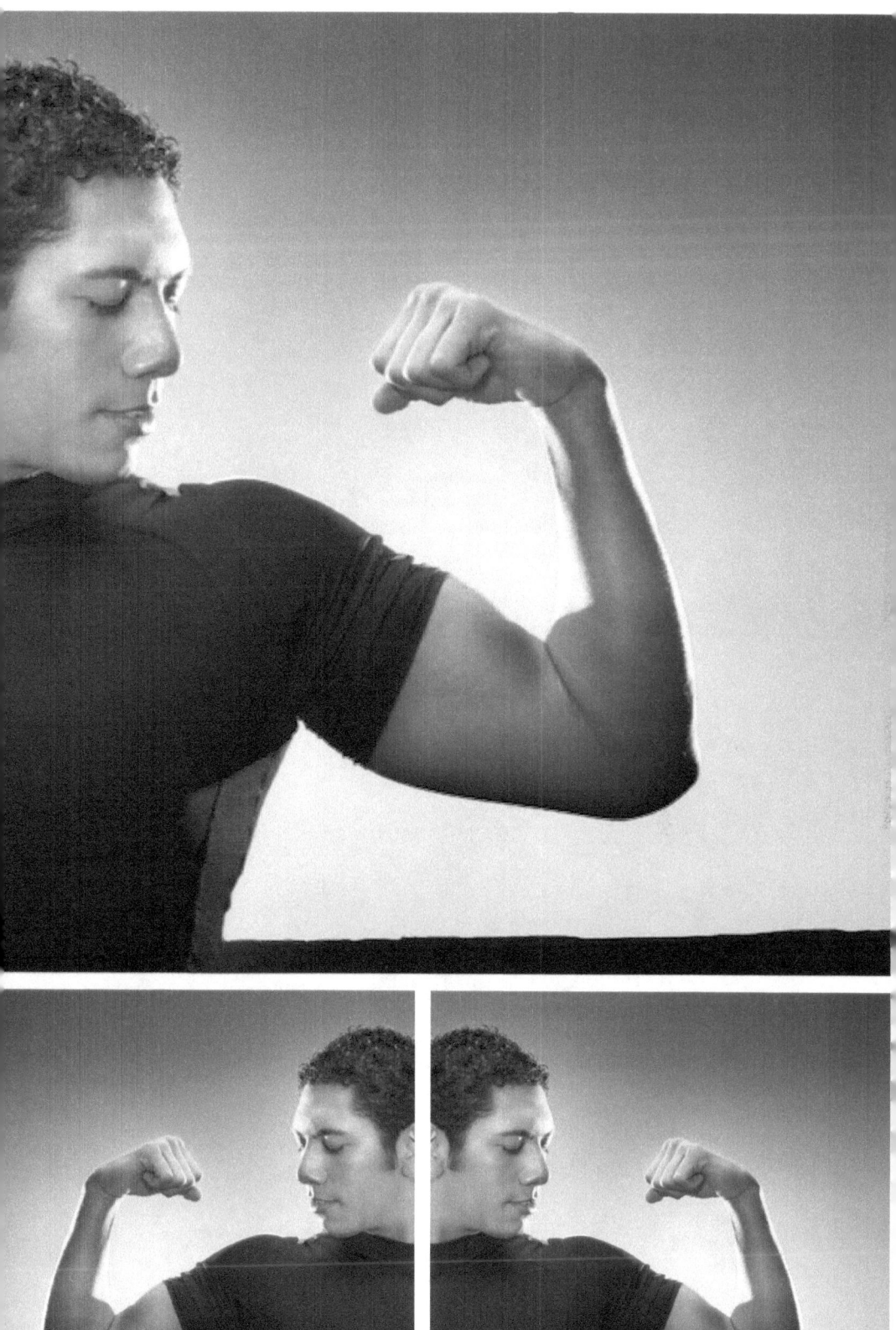

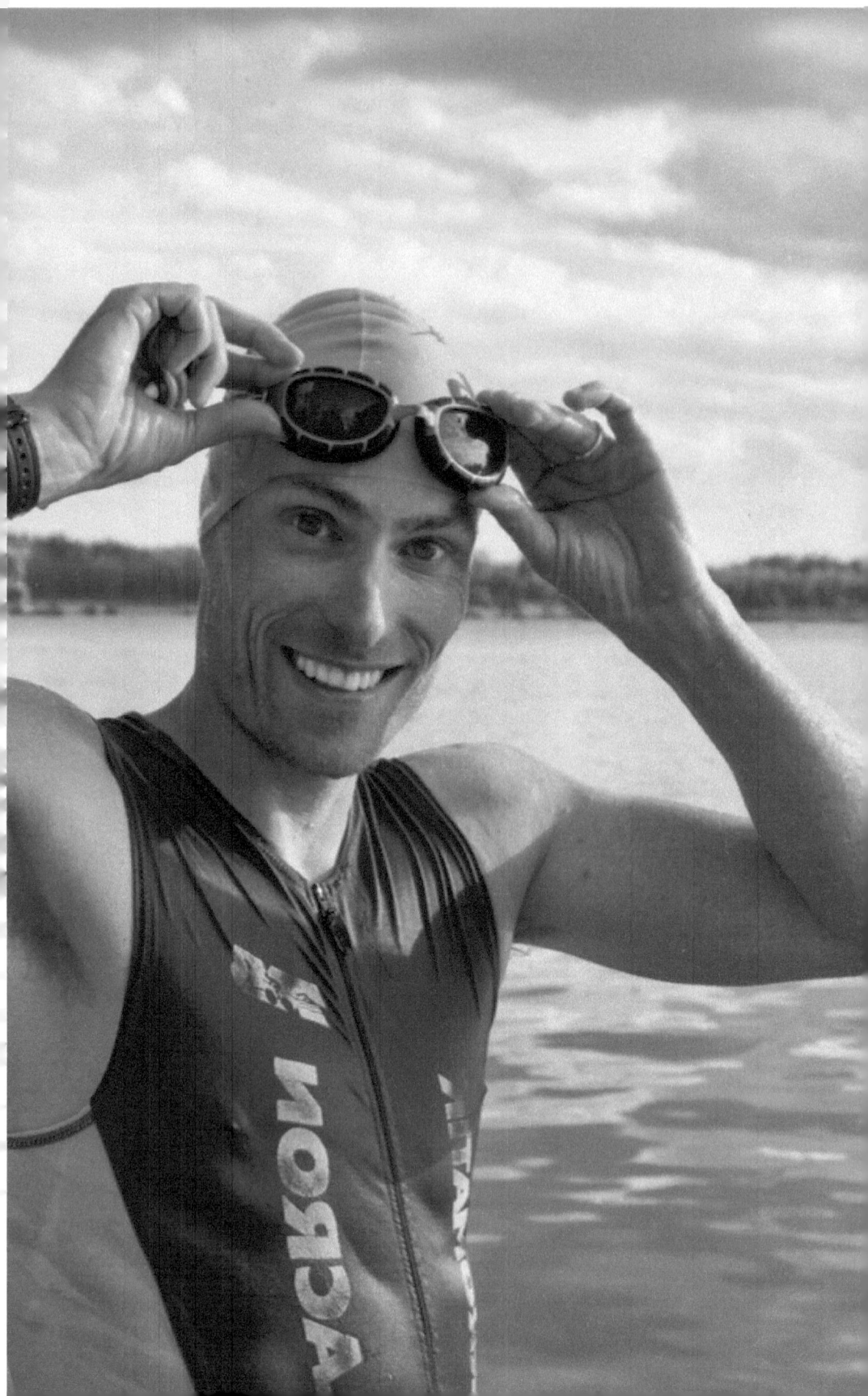

Never give up on a dream just because of the time it will take to accomplish it. The time will pass anyway.
Earl Nightingale

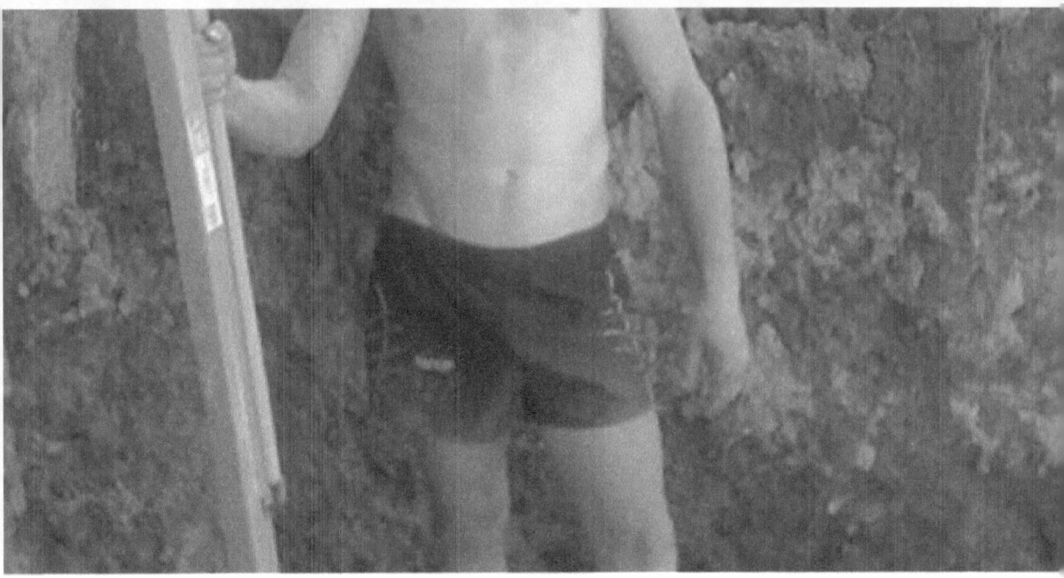

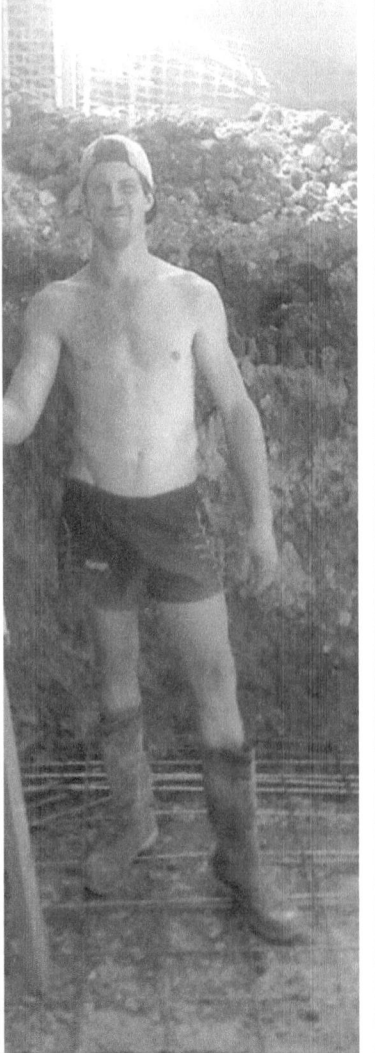

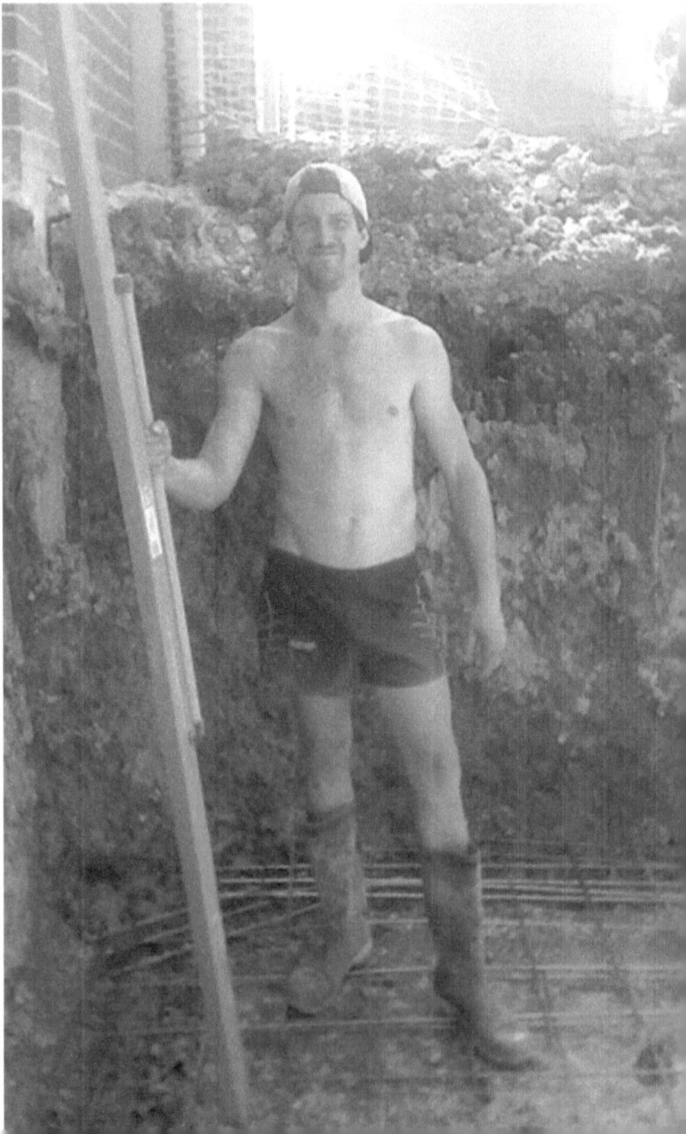

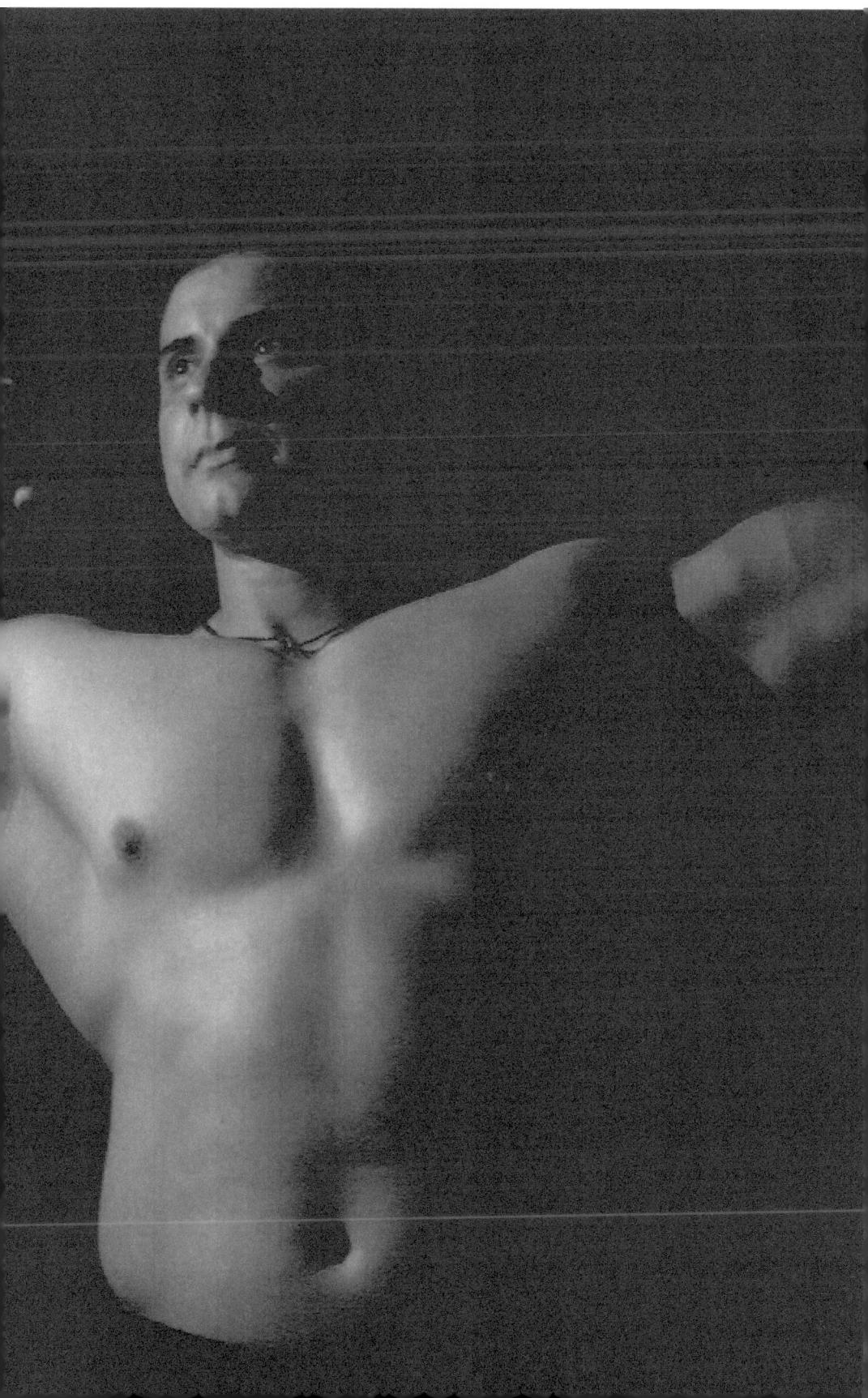

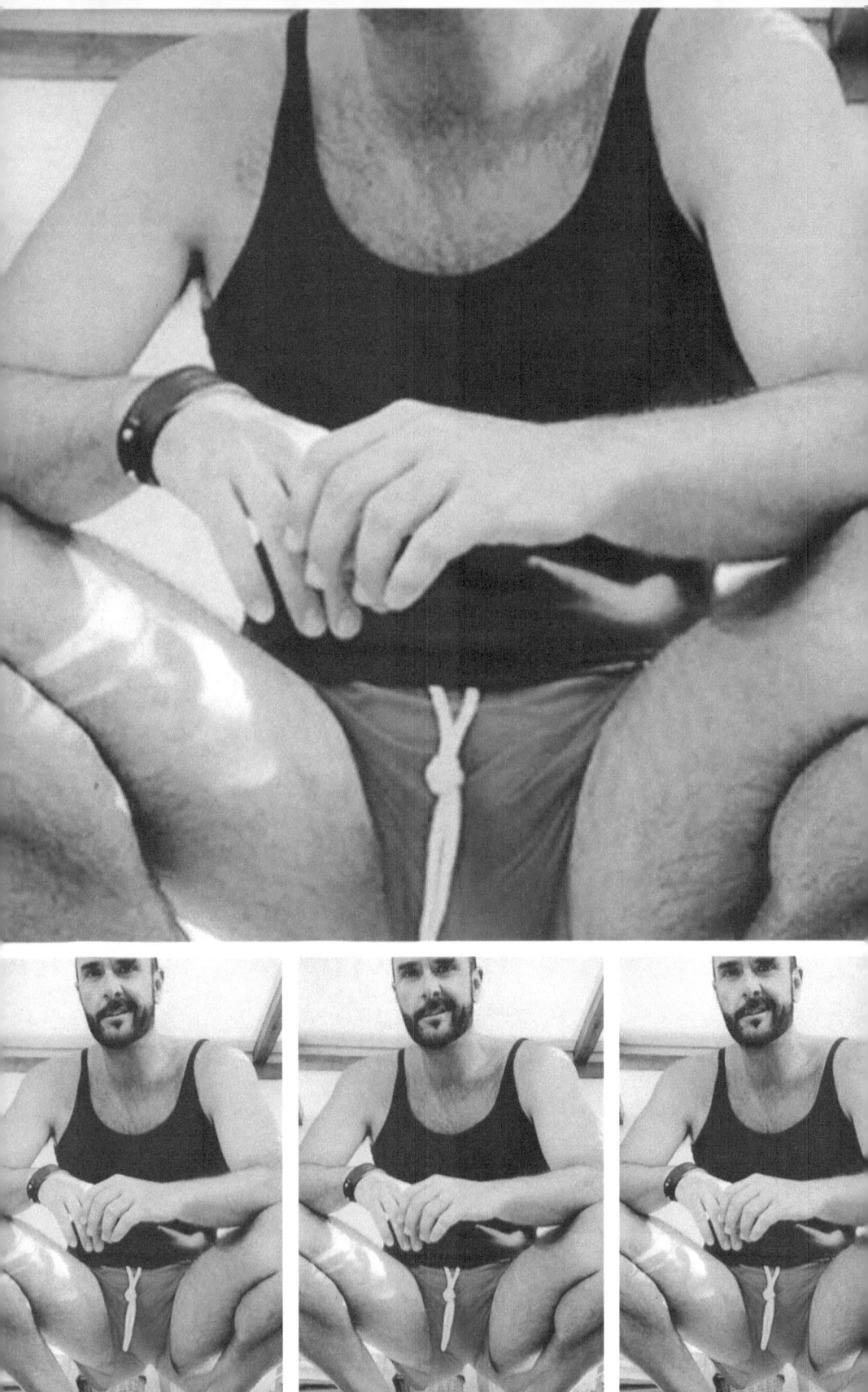

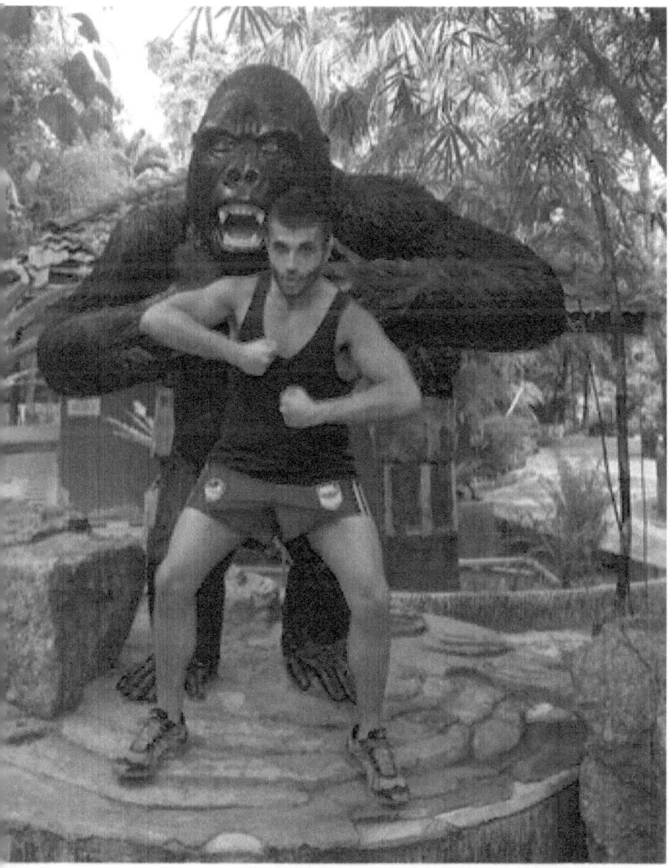

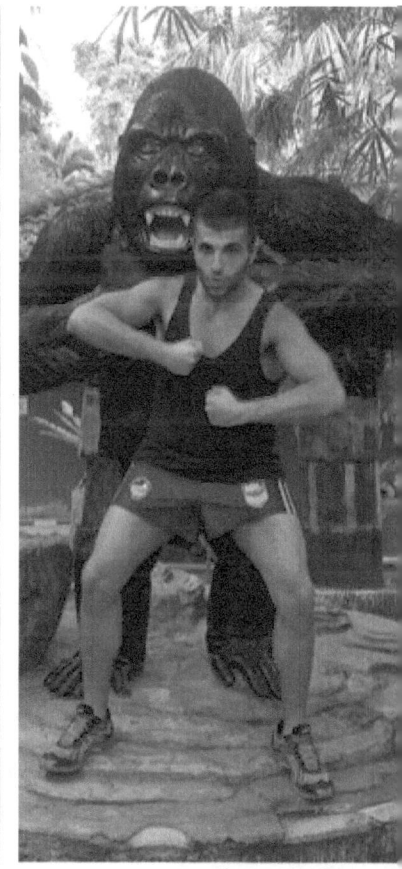
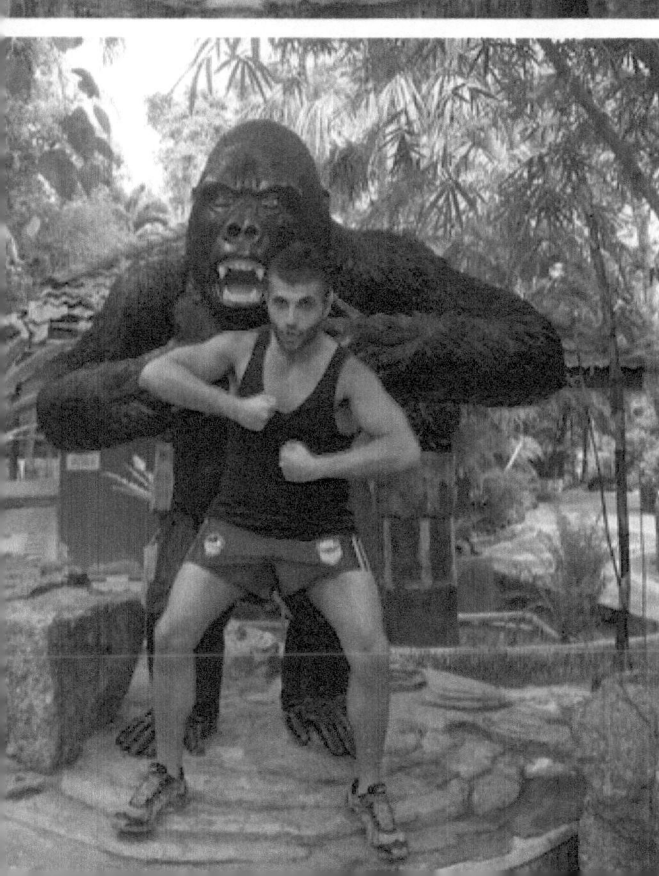
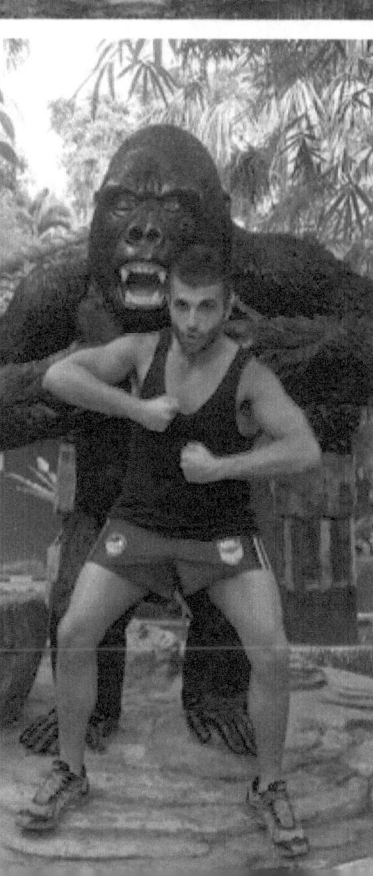